Listen to what others are saying!

"Choose Now to Grow Grand (Not Old) is a delightful read, filled with examples of women who have grown into maturity, some with grace to become grand ladies in their old age, and some who have reaped the rewards of bitterness and disappointment. Teri Gasser uses her artistic and insightful writing to guide the reader into thoughtful, biblical conclusions to use as models as they look forward to growing grand themselves." **Nancy Swihart**, Author of *On Kitten Creek: Searching for the Sacred*, retired Professor of English and Department Head of General Studies at Manhattan Christian College.

"Choose Now to Grow Grand, Not Old" highlights valuable life lessons author Teri Gasser learned from several grand women, centering on the power of our choices. The book was so filled with wisdom, wit and wonder, I couldn't put it down. Reading this gem reunited me with many dearly departed women I've been blessed to learn from. Read the stories, spend time pondering the "Choice Meditations, Choice Considerations, and Choice Actions" at the end of each chapter, and Choose Now to Grow Grand, Not Old," **Robin Shear**, Speaker, Joy Coach, Author of Messy Joy (coming in early 2023)

Choose Now to Grow Grand, Not Old:

12 Women over Eighty Show Us How to Smile at the Future

Choose Now to *Grow Grand,* Not Old

12 Women over Eighty Show Us How to Smile at the Future

by

†eri Gasser

SIT PRESS

A Publication of
Steeped In Truth Press

To my daughters, Rachel O'Neill, Jennifer Gasser, and Anna Standiford, I pray you will enjoy the preservation of these stories. By the examples set before us, let's grow grand together for the glory of God.

CONTENTS

Acknowledgments

As a reader, I glance at a book cover and see only one or two authors. As a first-time author, I now realize how many writers a book has. I am thankful to so many for their contribution to this work. First, to my Creator, Who writes all our stories. I am grateful for each woman named and unnamed in this book. Their influence has shaped me profoundly. I am thankful for the loving encouragement of my husband, Bill, and my daughters, who gave me feedback and made room in their homes for me to attend writer's conferences and have personal writer's retreats. I'm eternally grateful to my fellow Wellspring Writers: Nancy Swihart, Kay Bascom, Elena Shaw, and Jan Coles. These women not only listened to my rough drafts and rewrites but also love me, pray for me, and show me Jesus. To my team of prayer warriors, thank you for answering the call. I figured if God called you to pray, He called me to write. Thanks to Dana Krueger (one of those prayer warriors) for introducing me to a *fabulous* cover designer, Laura

Young. Thanks, Laura, for creating the perfect cover for this book. I appreciate Carol Kent encouraged me to take the writer's track at her Speak Up conference and wrote an endorsement for this book. I'm grateful for all my endorsers. Thanks to Cindy and Dave Lambert—to Cindy for her encouragement to pursue publication and to Dave for challenging me to work hard at writing better. I'm grateful to my excellent editors, Marjorie Vawter and Kristin Mctiernan, who patiently took me through the learning curves of book writing. Thanks also to Maria Estrada, my coworker who relentlessly asked, "How's the book coming?"

It's done, Maria. It's finally finished!

Preface

I have a friend with a photographic memory—a gift I certainly do not possess. My memories emerge from the fog of impressions. I feel an obligation to you, my reader, to be candid about the content of this book. Dialogues in this work are not verbatim quotes. Rather the quotation marks convey a general sense of actual conversations. I tend to have a good color memory, but I confess I may have gotten a few lines wrong. The tone or feeling those colors evoke is nonfiction. This book is not intended as a biography but rather to share impressions that continue to challenge my growth. There is also a pseudonym used for one person whose name I could not remember, even though I could describe him to you in great detail. I do hope if "Stan" or any of his relatives ever reads this book, they'll forgive my liberty with his name. Thank you for embarking on this journey with me.

1

Failing to Choose is Choosing to Fail

I have set before you life and death, blessings and curses. Now choose life.
Deuteronomy 30:19

Aging feels like an alien invasion. On the T.V. series, *Star Trek: The Next Generation,* an alien race called the Borg would arrive at a planet in a massive cubical starship and announce, "You will be assimilated. Resistance is futile." Getting old sounds the same.

No matter how we try to fight it or ignore it, we age. As time passes, gravity tugs at our physique. Hair and skin fade as vital pigment dissipates from our cells. As for me, six decades have marched over my body—and it shows.

Gravity took hold of my face, not to mention other pleasant features. Sag replaced firm. Wrinkled replaced smooth. Silver replaced gold (not a fair trade at all if you're talking about precious metals). And though I could color my hair, there's not enough elasticity in a spandex factory to recover from sixty years of planetary pull. Can you relate?

Even now, the invading force subtly but consistently announces, "You will be assimilated!" Old may sound ugly, but the fear of aging is uglier. The unnatural faces of aging actresses stretched like trampolines with Botox-puffed lips confirm this. What, you're not afraid of getting old? To quote Yoda, a more lovable alien, "You will be . . . *you will be!*"

Thoughts of losing our vitality, our independence—our minds—disturb us. Yes, sisters, there is a disturbance in the force! We dread the aches and pains of a failing body. We recoil at the thought of needing someone to help us with bathing or, worse yet, toileting. Will we let this fear enslave us or choose to conquer it?

If we give in to fear, we either condemn ourselves to depression or rebel in a ridiculous, futile struggle to undo the aging process. I see a better option—to bravely go where a few brave women have gone before. To face each day God gives by living as long as we're alive for His glory. We can *choose* to grow grand. But I warn you—this is not an easy choice.

God blessed me with good genes. Longevity runs on both sides of my family, particularly in women. I grew up knowing my grandmothers, great-grandmothers, and great-aunts. When I first drafted this chapter, my maternal grandmother was ninety-nine years old and still living alone in her apartment. Many of my relatives lived well into their nineties, and four were centenarians. Through these relationships, God gave me glimpses of His truth. He revealed to me the dos and don'ts of a grand life.

It doesn't matter where you are in life—young, middle-aged, or beyond—you need a plan to live well, especially if you live long. I often told my children, "Smart people learn from their mistakes. Smarter people learn from the mistakes of others." This principle applies to success also. The examples of others provide us with an excellent resource for living. However, finding examples of well-aged, *grand* people isn't easy. Good news! I know several grand women. In this book, I'll share the relationships that encouraged me to smile at the future and keep growing, not old but *grand*.

After turning twenty-five for the second time (you do the math), I realized I was well on my way to becoming an old woman. I became a grandmother that year. With that milestone came an epiphany: if we live long, we spend *most* of our lives as older people. I considered my earliest memories of my grandmothers. In my three-year-old eyes, they looked old. Yet, these two women were only forty-eight at that time. They were old as long as I knew them. The older I got, the older they got.

Facing the inevitable, I attended a workshop on finishing well. The speaker, a woman in her sixties, lamented the difficulty of finding older women to emulate. Her comments confirmed my suspicion—our generationally segregated society robs us of *role models*. Western culture, in particular, treats aging like a contagious disease, quarantining the elderly in nursing homes. Churches tend to congregate seniors in separate Bible studies and Sunday School classes. Worse yet, our busyness often keeps us from visiting women who no longer drive and find it hard to leave home. Older adults tend to be out of sight and out of mind.

The idea for this book bubbled in my brain for many years, but that day at the conference, God reminded me of all my role models, the many grandmothers I knew (I love that we call them *grand*mothers, not old mothers). God convinced me to get busy and write, to share what He was teaching me. As I wrote, I discovered how much I was still learning from these women and how their lives reflected God's wisdom.

Not all of these grand ladies followed Jesus, but God is no respecter of persons. He causes the rain to fall on the just and unjust alike (Matthew 5:45). When unregenerate people act right, they still receive a temporary blessing. Yes, even in the lives of unbelievers, God's goodness shines through at times. He used these women to captivate my heart, showing me the possibility of living a long and lovely life and how loveliness results from a series of well-made choices.

The contrasts between my grandmothers demonstrated to me the power of personal choice. They served as the original inspiration for this book. We all have the ability to choose. Either we make intentional choices to train our habits, or our habits take control of our choices. When we choose to form a new habit, it creates a good habit of choosing well. My grandmas' circumstances, values, and perspectives differed; so did their choices.

In the first section of this book, "The Grands," I begin by elaborating on the differences between my grandmothers. Then I share in greater detail their stories, so you will understand how choices trump circumstances in character development. This first section closes by contrasting how they each lived their last decade of life, and the *finale*—revealing the women they became through their choices.

In the second section, "The Greats," I'll introduce you to my "great" relatives—others who contributed to the gene pool of longevity I swim in. Four chapters make up this section. From the examples of two of my great-grandmothers and two of my great-aunts, I share what I'm learning about creating beauty, developing resilience, leaving a colorful legacy, and building friendships.

In the third section of my book, "The Guests," I introduce a neighbor, an acquaintance, and four mentors (from the three churches my husband pastored). Some of these relationships were close, others casual. Some occurred when I was a young woman, others recently. With seven to nine decades under their belts, these women influenced me. They displayed hospitality, vitality, courage, class, peace, and humility—indispensable qualities of a grand life.

The chapters in sections two and three are not in chronological order, so feel free to peruse the table of contents, as you would in a magazine, and read these chapters as you wish.

These vignettes of memory serve as illustrations, not detailed biographies. They formed lasting impressions. These women set intentional and unintentional examples. And in so doing, they loved me. They displayed timeless traits of imperishable beauty and lives well lived. Despite their age, they kept teaching, learning, and growing.

Living things grow. Growth serves as a major theme of this book. At the end of each chapter, you will find three growth opportunities to help you develop good choices. "Choice Meditations" are micro-Bible studies on the traits discussed in the chapter. "Choice Considerations" are self-examination questions designed to help you evaluate your current choices. Finally, "Choice Actions" suggests several application activities designed to help you grow better habits of choosing. Like an all-you-can-eat buffet, just pick what looks tasty.

Growing as an intellectual and spiritual being requires continuing education. I've designed these Choice Growth sections with lots of options for you to individualize your study plan. When we think we've seen and heard it all and stop receiving instruction, we quit growing. We die. The women in this book never die; they live in my heart. I want to grow up like them—I want to *grow grand*! Will you join me?

Part 1

The Grands

Contrasting My Two Grandmothers

2

The Tale of Two Grandmothers

Choose for yourselves this day whom you will serve.
Joshua 24:15

"I t was the best of times; it was the worst of times." Isn't family life like that? Families celebrate; they honor their heroes. Families endure tragedies and scandals; they blush over their odd ducks and black sheep. Irène and Erma—my grandmothers—shared three things in common. Both were born in the autumn of 1914; their children, my parents, fell in love and married; and they shared the world's second most fantastic grandchildren (mine are the greatest)—my brother and me. Beyond that, they were as different as roses and ragweed.

Grandmas come in all shapes and sizes. My mother's mom, Irène, was short and round with shapely legs. Her soft white hair framed her face and contrasted well with her olive skin. Even when almost blind, her dark eyes glowed like coals in the hearth, and her smile radiated with genuine cheer. Irène's irresistible countenance drew others in like a warm cabin on a cold day.

Erma, my father's mother, looked more like a tower than a cabin, her demeanor more imposing than inviting. With thick straight legs, she stood taller than Irène. Her dark hair hid the passing of time. A silver streak above her brow flowed through steel-gray hair. It remained dark salt and pepper until she died in her late nineties. Erma guarded her expressions, smiling only occasionally. Erma's eyes were also dark but sparkless. Her countenance resembled Eeyore's, always a bit down in the mouth.

Yes, Irène and Erma looked quite different—one *inviting*, the other *austere*. Irresistible Irène reminds me a bit of Winnie-the-Pooh, a honey-sweet soul radiating with sunshine and friendliness. "Any day spent with you is my favorite day," Pooh told his playmate. Grandma Irène often expressed similar thoughts to her company. Erma resembled another A.A. Milnes character. She embraced the sentiments of Eeyore: "The sky has finally fallen. Always knew it would." Erma often seemed down in the mouth and under a cloud.

Irresistible Irène was born and raised on the East Coast; Eeyore Erma was born and raised on the west. Irresistible Irène was the oldest child; Eeyore Erma was the youngest. Irène grew up in an orphanage after her father passed away; Erma grew up with both her parents. Irène grew up dirt poor; Erma grew up well-off. Irène completed the eighth grade; Erma earned a two-year college degree. Irène, a single mom, worked two jobs; Erma, a well-kept wife, worked as a full-time homemaker. Irène worshipped as a Catholic, and Erma as a Protestant. I could go on and on contrasting these two, but then I'd never get to the point of this book. Their differences revealed to me *the power of choices*.

Our *choices*—not our circumstances—account for who we become. Circumstances shape us, but choices define us. Some of us contend with more significant challenges than others; sometimes, our greatest challenge is *ourselves*. Will we indulge in the world's folly and follow our hearts? Scripture reminds us this is a *bad* choice. "Our hearts are deceitful above all things and desperately wicked" (Jeremiah 17:9). Will we choose to respond with raw emotion or self-control? Will we give in, give up, or get through? We are who we are because that's who *we chose* to be. Our choices forge our character and determine the quality of our lives.

Shakespeare's line in *Hamlet* resonates in much of life: "To be or not to be? That is the question." Everyday variations of that question confront us. To work or not to work? To help or not to help? To forgive or not to forgive? To smile or not to smile? To speak or not to speak? As a constant parade of people, possibilities, problems, pain, and perplexities marches through our lives, we choose how to engage or disengage with each. Through that process of choosing, we become our future selves. What kind of people do we want to be? Kind? Patient? Wise?

King Solomon, purportedly the wisest man who ever lived, wrote, "The end of a matter is better than the beginning" (Ecclesiastes 7:8). We've heard it countless times because it's true; it's not how we start but how we *finish*. If we wrote our epitaph, what would we want it to say? We need to start making choices now with that end in mind.

My Great Aunt Lola (Erma's older sister) threw herself a birthday party when she turned ninety. Her oldest sister, Alba, gave her a card with the blessing, "May you live as long as you want to, and want to as long as you do." Lola got it! But Erma did not. Erma lived longer than she wanted to, failing to appreciate her last years of life.

On the contrary, Erma's sisters, Lola and Alba, seemed content with their daily lives. Erma lived close to family, a privilege Lola and Alba never enjoyed. Yet, they appreciated life more than their younger sister. Erma sank into a deep depression after her son's (my father) unexpected death at sixty-seven. Her bitter laments alienated her eldest son, who visited her every week. Her choice to wallow in self-pity grieved us all.

On the other hand, my grandma, Irène, celebrated her one-hundredth birthday with all of her children, most of her grandchildren, and many other relatives. Many traveled from out of state, and a few from across the country. Many residents of North Plains, Oregon came too. Irène spent the last decade of her life in that small Oregon community. Her new friends paid her visits until the day she died. Irène never grew old. Her body wore out, but her spirit *grew grand*. She aged well.

A decorative tin sign hangs in my kitchen. It reads, "Attitude is everything. Pick a good one." I need this constant reminder to choose my attitudes carefully. I love the way Howard Hendricks said, "Your attitude affects your altitude." Up or down, smile or frown, joy or disillusionment, peace or anger—these choices lay lines on a countenance and mark a face for all to see. We live in a fallen world, but our attitudes don't have to crash and burn with it. Imagine the smell of smoke from a plane crash: burning fuel, hot metal, smoldering plastic. Do we want attitudes that stink? Choice empowers us to rise above our circumstances.

Grandmother One

I grew up as a Navy brat, so we seldom lived near extended family. On a few occasions, I lived in the same state as each of my grandmothers, and for a brief period, I even lived under their roofs. My parents and I resided with my dad's folks for the first year of my life, which was too early for me to remember. The year I began kindergarten, we lived with my maternal grandma, Irène. My mind keeps a scrapbook of pleasant memories from that short stay. But most visits to my grandparents required us to travel. We traveled hours, if not days, to spend time with them. As a result, we showed up with more baggage than just the suitcases. The fatigue and stress of travel tagged along.

Irène knew how to unpack that baggage. She embraced us as we were—children. Irène lavished us with hugs and kisses and played with my brother and me. She showed interest in us. She praised our accomplishments and corrected us in love. Her genuine affection drew us in.

When blotting her lipstick, Irène preferred a child's cheek to a tissue. My mother hated this like I detested my mom licking her finger to get a smudge off my face. I, on the other hand, loved Grandma Irène's lip prints. After my Grandma kissed my cheek, I'd run to the mirror. What a thrill, at five years old, to gaze on my reflection and see that dark, pink smooch stamped there branding me as her *grand*child!

Not only did Irène make lip prints on our faces, but she created other things too. You name it; Irène crocheted it: hats, vests, fun pillow coverings (a teddy bear pillow for my brother and a doll one for me), and even a beautiful yellow dress for me. Irène also designed fabulous ball gowns for my Barbie dolls with her skeins of yarn.

Grandma Irène allowed me to explore her jewelry box, a treasure chest of rhinestones and bobble brooches, necklaces, and clip-on earrings. This privilege sparked my young imagination. Grandma's jewels transformed me into a princess and a pirate. I remember my all-time favorite dress-up, Grandma Irène's fluffy, white can-can slip. The yards of layered tulle and lace transformed me into a royal bride. Irène added sparkle by sharing her costume jewelry. She and I shared a thing for bling; I loved donning her rhinestones. I also loved eating her sweet treats.

When mom and I lived with her while my dad went through OCS (Officer Candidate School), Irène took me to church every Sunday, something new to me. My parents didn't go, but my mom let Grandma take me. She never forced me. I enjoyed going with her. It was my first introduction to Christianity. She bought me a red velvet beret. "Teri, you need a hat to wear to church," she told me. It was the sixties, after all, and Irène loved being trendy.

Photos confirm her fashion awareness. One taken in the late sixties shows her sporting a fabulous beehive updo.

Once my dad completed OCS, we moved to South Carolina. After my sixth birthday, the Navy deployed my daddy to Vietnam. Christmas time rolled around. It was our first Christmas without him. My mom and I flew to Connecticut to visit Grandma Irène for the holiday, hoping for a distraction from Daddy's absence. Irène showed me her nativity while telling me the story of Advent. Then she cautioned me to be careful and let me play with the figures.

Later that week, Irène took us to the top of the G. Foxes' department store to see the Christmas light display. The roof of that fourteen-story building had morphed into a winter wonderland of illumination—a wondrous sight to behold—especially for the very young! I wandered through the lights, amazed by the glory of it: Santa's elves and sleigh complete with reindeer, trumpeting angels, stars, and a crèche. To my young soul, it seemed like a glimpse of heaven.

My mom promised I could open one gift on Christmas Eve when Grandma came home from midnight mass. The scents of pine and warm wax from the lit candles greeted us as we gathered around the tree. My grandma handed me her present. The small box tinkled when I shook it. I'd been told the best gifts come in small packages. I ripped off the wrapping and lifted the lid of the tiny velvet box. It was the prettiest brooch I'd ever seen. Real grown-up jewelry! Two little brass bells hung from deep green holly leaves and a shiny red berry. I still wear this brooch every year at Christmas. Its bells ring with the magic of that Christmas with Grandma Irène, the Christmas that consoled a little Navy brat who missed her daddy.

Irène chose to hold us and take time for us. She chose to give and share, to love even when, as a teen, I was not very lovable. I remember her serious tone during one visit when I was fifteen. "Teri, come upstairs. I need to talk to you."

I followed her without hesitation. When we entered the bedroom, she motioned me to sit on the bed. I did. "Why do you hate your mother so much?" She asked me point-blank.

Stunned, I retorted, "I don't hate her!"

"The way you speak to her is hateful. The way you roll your eyes at her is hateful. You can say you don't hate her, but your actions say otherwise." I listened in shame as she continued, "Your mother is my daughter, and I love her very much. She works hard to make a good home for you. She is not perfect, but she does not deserve the disrespect you show her. It hurts me when I see you treat her that way, and I don't want to see any more of it. Do you understand?" Her eyes made steady contact with mine the whole time she spoke. She expected an answer.

"I'm sorry, Grandma."

"As you should be; now, go tell your mom." She leaned over and held me, kissing me on the forehead.

Her correction got my attention far better than a lecture or grounding from my mother ever could have.

Irène not only practiced tough love and chose presents well, but she also gave her presence—the best gift anyone could give. She made the choices that the best grandmothers have always made. Decisions that make them grand!

Grandmother Two

My dad's mother, Erma, made different choices. Traveling to visit her for Christmas one year, I could sense the growing tension as we drove closer to her house.

"Shoot, gosh darn, shoot gosh, darn..." I whispered under my breath, over and over, as we drove along in the family sedan. My arms itched under a slather of thick, pink Calamine lotion. I had broken out in hives. Despite my urgent appeals and tantrums, we traveled north to my father's parents' home in Porterville, California. I was thirteen. I wanted to spend my Christmas break at home, hanging out with my friends. This trip felt like being exiled to Siberia. Given a choice between Erma's and Siberia, I would have chosen Siberia—at least they have a white Christmas.

"Teri," Mom's stern tone caught my immediate attention as we backed out of the driveway. "You watch your tongue at Grandma Donaldson's. She hates swearing, and she better not hear any from you!"

I continued chanting euphemisms for miles, not as a protest but as practice. I needed to replace my unsavory words to keep from embarrassing my folks. At the tender age of nine, my mom told me she didn't care what words I used, permitting me to swear. My father was a sailor. My mother was French. By junior high, I spewed out a vocabulary that could make a biker blush. My grandmother, Erma, on the other hand, took great offense at coarse superlatives. And my dad and mom wanted peace and acceptance from this woman whose approval was difficult to secure.

This pressure sucked the joy out of our visits—all that anxiety to avoid one woman's condescension and consternation. Had I been going to Grandma Irène's for Christmas, I'd have broken out in song. Going to Erma's caused me to break out in hives, hence the calamine lotion. Her disapproval felt like rejection. Erma failed to communicate unconditional love.

God's unconditional love leads the lost to salvation. Did she want us to be saved, changed? Maybe she was lost too; lost in her self-righteousness, lost in her religion with no relationship to Jesus? I can't say I ever saw Erma display the compassion or love of Christ. Once in a while, I heard her talk about going to church, though she never invited me. And I never heard her speak about Jesus. So, there I sat in the back seat, mumbling to myself as we descended under Erma's foreboding cloud.

Erma had a strange way of motivating my dad and his brothers. She would play them against each other, bragging about one to the other. All three of her sons thought one of the others was her favorite. Years of competition and envy alienated the brothers, breeding resentment towards one another—and their mom—because they felt they could never please her. Late in life, the brothers became wise to her strategy, but they never overcame the rivalry that separated them.

To be fair, I think she intended to teach them humility and diligence. Instead, their inability to gain her approval cultivated bitterness. All my growing up years, my father dreaded visiting his mother. His dread led to our discomfort.

Erma cared little for physical shows of affection. This left my father, whose love language was touch, with an empty love cup as a boy. My poor father suffered from terrible ear infections as a toddler. The repeated illness resulted in mastoid surgery when he was two. Erma left him to cry out much of his pain, rarely holding him or rocking him to give him comfort.

She chided my mom for picking me up when I cried, saying, "You'll just spoil her if you pick her up every time she cries." My mom ignored her and tended to my needs, even if it was just a need for attention. My mom and dad's hugs were always warm and satisfying, but Erma's hugs felt stiff and awkward. She kissed me with quick pecks that seldom made full contact with my face. No lip prints left on my cheek like Irène always left.

During most of our visits with my dad's folks, Erma spent the time in her sewing room, visiting with my mother. After passing out a few old toys to my brother and me and a "honey-do" list to my dad, she and my mom disappeared into her mysterious workroom. It may as well have had a sign stating "no children allowed" because Erma barely acknowledged me on the rare occasions I entered. She expected my mom to deal with me.

My mom tells me their conversations revolved around local gossip about people she didn't know and sewing tips. Erma did teach my mom how to sew. I think that's why she sewed so little for me. She expected my mother should do it. Erma, a skilled seamstress, made me one tailored suit when I was in my early twenties. On rare occasions, she created a dress for my Barbie doll from scraps.

My fondest memories are of her homemade cookies and canned apricots, but those were a staple in her home—not special treats for grandchildren. Nor did she distribute those tasty morsels liberally. Erma doled out a modest dessert as a privilege for those who cleaned their supper plate. Seconds on dessert were not an option. To her credit, I do remember one Christmas she sent me some of her home-dried apricots because she knew I enjoyed them.

The highlight of those trips to my dad's folks was the time spent with my grandpa, not Erma. I always enjoyed supper time at Erma's. I would sit by my grandpa. He and I played a little game. He'd walk his fingers up my arm and say, "The spider's going to get you!"

I'd laugh and slap at his hand, missing it as he'd pull it away, asking, "Why are you hitting yourself?"

His affectionate games and jokes made our visits fun but did not compensate for Erma's neglect. Having observed her as a great-grandmother to my kids, I don't think she enjoyed the company of children. She treated them as objects to be seen, not people to interact with.

Both of my grandmothers lived on middle-class incomes, but my dad's parents had more than my mom's. Yet when it came to gift-giving, Irène gave generously. Erma, not so much. When I was in high school, Grandma Irène's card always contained a twenty-dollar bill. Erma still chose to give me one dollar as she had my whole life. Irène had a dozen grandchildren to gift, Erma only four. Erma budgeted eight dollars a year for grandchildren—one for birthdays and one for Christmas. Even back in the sixties and seventies, this sum reeked of stinginess.

Erma's husband, my grandpa, would, on occasion, take me to a toy store and let me pick a toy to take home. No doubt he knew his wife was tight-fisted, but he liked keeping the peace. So, he let her budget us each two bucks a year.

Please, understand my motive for exposing Erma in this manner. I don't believe you should buy your grandchildren's love. I simply want to contrast the choices they made regarding generosity. However, I confess that opening Irène's card was always more fun.

Irène quit sending us birthday money after we graduated from high school. She knew her fixed income required some restraint if she was going to indulge her great-grandchildren someday. On the other hand, Erma gave me a dollar even after I had my children. By the nineties, one dollar covered the cost of a stamp and thank-you card, an appropriate response to all gifts. And so, I dutifully spent the dollar and sent a thank you to Erma. At least the irony of her gift gave me a chuckle.

Once when I was a young, single woman, Erma traveled to Tacoma by train to visit me. I brought her to the salon where I worked. Then I treated her to dinner at an upscale restaurant. We seemed to be having a good time. I loved my grandmother Erma, and I longed for her approval. I guess I was hoping for a closer, more satisfying relationship, like the one I enjoyed with Irène. I hoped Erma had enjoyed herself and getting to know me that evening.

She left the following day to visit my folks in Idaho. After her visit there, my mother told me about Erma's disapproval of my *wild hairstyle*. "You'd think as a professional cosmetologist, Teri would have a pretty hairstyle!"

I did have an attractive hairstyle. Women regularly stopped me on the street to pay compliments and ask where I had my hair done. It just wasn't *Erma's* style, so, in her opinion, it was the wrong style. I had failed to live up to her expectations again. Her disappointment stung. She dashed my expectations as well.

It became clear that to continue to love her meant I must choose *not* to expect her to change. I had to take our relationship as it was. I couldn't strive to keep pleasing her. I just needed to accept the fact that Erma was hard to please and love her anyway.

Erma chose to expect a lot from people and life in general. She also chose to voice her disappointment. Her poor habits of choice alienated those she claimed to love.

Thumbing through old family photos, looking at pictures of my grandmothers and me, I made an interesting observation; for the first time, I noticed in most of the images with Grandma Irène that she was looking and smiling at me. She's also snuggling me close. In the photos of Grandma Erma and me, Erma is looking at the camera, not paying any attention to me. Pictures confirmed what I had always felt. Irène cared about me. Erma cared about appearances.

The film captured the fruit of their choices. Irène chose to focus on others. Erma focused on expectations. How had their habits of choosing formed? How did they become the grandmothers they were? What made Irène irresistible and clouded Eeyore Erma's countenance?

Choice Meditations

Throughout the book of Proverbs, contrasts are used as a teaching tool. Examine the following proverbs: 12:1; 13:4; 14:1, 29–30; 15:1–2, 13, 19.

1. What contrast is made in each?

2. In light of these contrasts, write a personal commitment to make a specific good choice from each proverb. For example, in Proverbs 12:1, the next time someone corrects me, I will choose to listen and learn with humility.

Choice Considerations

1. How do my children and grandchildren or younger friends view our time together? Am I a blessing to them more often than not? Get brave and ask them!

2. What is one thing I can choose to do regularly that will make a fond memory for my grandchild or a friend of a younger generation?

3. Do I show physical affection? (Remember, it may not be something you enjoy, but something they need.)

Choice Actions

1. Buy or make some cards for family members or friends. Write them a few personal notes of encouragement throughout the year. Tell how you pray for them, thank them, and share what you find a blessing about them.

2. Put together a special treat basket for a family member or friend next time they visit from out of town. If they are local, surprise them with a treat basket. It can be as simple as homemade goodies.

3. Compliment someone every day.

4. Give lots of hugs, kisses, praise, and pats on the back.

3

The Knitter and the Golden Thread

A man's pride will bring him low, but the humble in spirit will retain honor.
Proverbs 29:23

T he heroine and antagonist in the *Tale of Two Cities* remind me of my two grandmothers. Erma possessed Madame Defarge's pride. Hence, she often lived low—under the clouds. Irène displayed Lucie Manette's redemptive ability to be gracious; her pleasant dispositions allowed her to live sunny-side-up.

The Early Life of Eeyore Erma

Erma Beatrice Burton came into the world on November 12, 1914. For her mother, Sadie, this time of year brought sorrow. In the fall, three years before, Sadie suffered the death of her firstborn, Pauline. Sadie delivered Erma under the cloud of this painful loss. Sadie's two surviving daughters greeted Erma: Alba, age four and a half, and Lola, just three. Erma remained the youngest child of the Burton family.

Sadie probably felt overwhelmed by the demands of three young daughters. Had Pauline lived, she would have been eight—such a helpful age. I suspect if Erma had been a boy, Sadie would have felt differently. But no! Erma was just another girl—born under a cloud of grief.

Erma's father, Michael, grew up in the Catholic church and immigrated to America when he was sixteen. He worked as a fireman (shoveled coal into the engine furnace) for the Union Pacific Railroad, but he was an American dreamer. He purchased a homestead in rural southern Idaho before he married Sadie.

The Union Pacific ran a rail through the mountains and wheat fields of the region. The tracks ran right past Erma's childhood home in Virginia, Idaho. This proximity allowed Michael to continue working on the railroad and start farming. This excerpt from Erma's memoir describes her mother's plight.

> "Mom was entirely out of her element—no social whirl, no neighbors for a while. She had many inconveniences to put up with. They had a cow so she would skim the cream off the shallow pans of milk and churn butter. The wooden butter churn was still around and used in my day. She would sit and churn and cry for all the things she had given up."

As a younger woman, did my great-grandmother complain a lot? My folks and I never heard her complain. Complaints in a home rise into clouds of discontent. Were these the clouds hanging over Erma's countenance?

Despite these clouds, Erma enjoyed an idyllic childhood filled with pets, camping, and fishing trips. Sadie taught her girls how to sew. They cut many outgrown dresses into quilt pieces. The Burton girls enjoyed quilting together. Erma also liked cooking, the 4-H club, and attending county and state fairs. She loved Old Burt, the pony she rode everywhere, and the stray dog, Jack, she adopted as a pet. Jack gained local celebrity status when Erma taught him to run down the dusty road for about a quarter-mile to retrieve the daily paper. Erma enjoyed both the attention of neighbors and Jack's affection.

Michael worked hard so his girls could play. He built a teeter-totter and swing for his girls. I'll let Erma fill you in on a few more details.

"In 1924 our family and the Marshall family went on a great tour of Yellowstone Park in two Model T Fords. Daddy built a cupboard for the left running board, and there was a board from fender to fender for the pup tent and bedding. In the back seat was more stuff, mostly under our feet. What a fine time we had. We caught trout for supper every day. We had never been to the high country before and it was a little scary in some places. The animals were in great abundance.

When we got back, Daddy built a playhouse and used the pup tent for a roof. I was nailing some lath for the sides when I dropped the hammer on my beautiful china head doll and smashed it to smithereens! I cried and cried, but the family all commiserated with me. The next Christmas, they gave me a larger doll."

Clouds of Comparison

Like most babies in a family, Erma looked up to her older siblings. Alba had her mother's looks, fair-haired and blue eyes. Lola took after her dad, with deep brown curls and dark eyes. Erma, with her dark brown eyes and straight brown hair, never thought she was as pretty as her big sisters. She also felt fat. Her impression resulted from comparing her average frame to her petite sisters. I've seen pictures of the young Erma; she was not fat.

Alba was mamma's pet. She helped in the house. Lola excelled as daddy's girl. She loved ranch life, caring for animals, and tending the field. Erma felt she needed to compete for attention.

Erma's tendency to compare and compete with her sisters produced an unhealthy self-image. Comparison steals our contentment. Even worse, it leads to depression. Sadly, Erma didn't understand this.

Erma and her sisters once won a 4-H trophy for their canning skills. Lola Burton, the middle sister's name, appeared on top. Engraved below her name came Alba, followed by a ditto mark, then Erma, and another ditto. The inscription irked Erma. "My name is not Erma ditto!" she protested, "The judges need to make a new trophy!"

"Now, Erma, there's no need to complain. You won." Responded her mother.

"But I'm not a ditto!" she kept insisting.

Erma's insistence persisted until her dying days. Eighty years after the fact, she recited to me her well-rehearsed grievance. Time failed to temper her discontent. The trophy sits in my china cupboard. It reminds me not to get my knickers in a knot when I feel overlooked. It's not worth the energy and doesn't change the dittos.

At sixteen, Erma had a steady boyfriend, Reed Thomas, the son of a wealthy rancher. Not a bad catch for a plain, fat girl. After high school, she found a new love interest, Max Donaldson. Her sisters were going on a double date. The men planned to take the girls to a local swimming resort, but neither owned a vehicle. Their boss, Max, agreed to drive them down in his old Ford. Rather than making Max the fifth wheel, they asked Erma to join them. Max found Erma fetching. And I suspect Erma took pleasure in the fact that her date was the boss of her sisters' boyfriends.

Once fall came, Erma headed north to Pocatello, Idaho, to attend college. Shortly after her arrival, Max came calling, and they started dating. A few weeks later, her old boyfriend, Reed, showed up driving his *brother's* brand-new Buick.

"Why do you want to go out with a man in an old, beat-up Ford?" Erma's landlord asked. "You could have a guy in a fine, new Buick."

Erma liked the Buick and Reed's wealthy family, but he was a rancher with no intention of leaving Downey, Idaho. Erma preferred Max, a well-educated, ambitious engineer. A man, not a boy, who *owned* his car. He was going somewhere in life, somewhere beyond rural Idaho.

Clouds of Perfectionism

Erma embraced the cultural opportunities of college life. She became involved with the theater program as their seamstress. Her sewing led to an invitation from the drama sorority Delta Psi Omega; Erma joined. Max gave her a ruby and pearl brooch to commemorate the occasion. Erma treasured his gift. An artist at heart, she had an eye for beauty.

One of Erma's pen-and-ink drawings hangs in my library. She depicted fairies riding on butterflies and bees, with elves in the garden below. Her signature, neat and tight, reveals her pursuit of perfection. "Erma Beatrice Burton" hand-printed in 8-point font arches over the completion date. Her distinctive signature—legible and beautiful—embellishes the picture. She penned it when she first started dating Max. She felt pretty pleased with it until she showed it to him.

"What do you think?" Erma asked Max.

Being an engineer, Max subconsciously counted the wings and legs of the creatures in the picture.

"The bee has seven legs," he stated, matter-of-factly, intending no harm. The simple fact so devastated Erma's opinion of her work that she never drew with ink again. Fortunately, she kept the piece hidden in a drawer. Years later, Erma pulled it out after Max died and showed it to my mom.

"It's lovely. Why don't you draw anymore?" inquired my mom.

My mom didn't notice the extra leg until Erma pointed it out and recounted Max's comment. My mom framed the drawing and hung it in her home, later passing it on to me. Even with a seven-legged bee, Erma's creation enchants me.

Erma overlooked Max's art critique, and the two married in 1934. Their first child arrived fourteen months later; Max named the infant Robert after his older brother, who died as a young man of eighteen. Three years later, son number two (my father), David, arrived. She longed to sew pretty dresses but stitched lots of shirts instead. Plaids and pockets replaced the calicos and ruffles of Erma's youth. I heard she dressed my dad in pink the first year of his life because she wanted a girl so badly.

Erma felt ill-equipped for babies, particularly boys. As the baby of a family growing up with few neighbors nearby, she had no experience with infants. I found this reflection in her memoir;

"I had never been around babies, so I had to learn everything the hard way. I did have a college text,

Home and Hygiene. We struggled through, but it wasn't easy. I took Bob, and later Dave, monthly to a caring pediatrician and he advised me well. Their formulas were stabilized after weeks of trying. Bob was never fat, but Dave was.

If you rated mothers one to ten, undoubtedly, I'd be a six. With age comes a little wisdom. I wasn't ready to be a mother. I sincerely wish I had been a better parent, and I'm sorry for my sins of omission and commission."

Reading Erma's memoir, I found no evidence that she relied on grace. To receive grace from God and understand His grace enables us to extend grace to others. Poor Erma missed out.

As World War II began, Max went to enlist. The physician who examined him rated him 4F due to the disabilities caused by polio. Instead of going off to war, Erma's husband stayed home. The war effort opened the door to a new opportunity for Max. ALCOA Aluminum hired him as a surveyor to build a new plant in Spokane, WA. Erma and Max packed up and headed six hundred miles northeast with their young sons, ages four and one. Good riddance, southern Idaho!

The Inland Empire, comprised of eastern Washington, Northern Idaho, and western Montana, provides an endless playground for folks who love the great outdoors. Max and his boys were outdoorsmen. Hiking, fishing, and camping became highlights of my father's early childhood. But for Erma, the pleasure of roughing it faded. The bride of Max's youth, who seemed to share his love of the outdoors, was not the woman he found himself married to.

Disappointments confront everyone. Someone we love will fail to live up to our expectations. The challenge is to keep on loving them. Erma and Max met the challenge. Max and Erma had a good marriage, albeit not a perfect one.

Erma never enjoyed the freedom that comes with abandoning perfectionism. She failed to recognize idealism as her foe. The cloud of perfectionism overshadowed her until the day she died.

Settling Under a Cloudy Contentment

Seven years after David was born, Erma bore her third and final child, my uncle Bruce, another boy. Bruce came on the heels of the family's last major move.

For several years, Max worked two weeks on the day shift and then two weeks on the swing shift. The shift changes wreaked havoc on his body. Childhood polio left him handicapped. He looked for another job and landed a position as a surveyor in Porterville, California. The move came in the last trimester of Erma's pregnancy. Her parents came down to help them get settled in. By this time, Erma had found new confidence in her parenting. She nursed Bruce for a year and found him to be a happy, chubby baby. No doubt, her growth allowed Bruce to thrive.

Max and Erma became lifelong residents of Porterville. The three boys took music lessons and played ball. All three graduated from Porterville High School, located right across the street from their house. Erma joined the PTA and grew a tailoring business at home; she altered and sewed for clients well into her seventies. With various fruit trees in their yard, Erma canned the apricots and dried the walnuts and pecans. Every Christmas, she'd candy the nuts she harvested from her yard. Years flew by as she made peanut butter and jelly sandwiches (a Donaldson favorite), packed lunches, attended church, cooked, and sewed. Her boys grew and flew. She settled into her empty nest.

She and Max had only a few friends—plenty for a couple of introverts. She yearned to travel, but Max's health prevented it. Despite their differences, they fulfilled their nuptial vows for forty-two years. After becoming a well-provided-for widow at age sixty-four, she pursued her passion, becoming quite a globe trotter.

In her memoir, Erma writes about her trips in detail. Over the next two decades, she traveled to all fifty of the United States and numerous countries spanning six of the seven continents. After enduring many Idaho winters, she had no interest in seeing Antarctica.

Erma was grateful for her opportunity to see the world. Her countenance lifted when she spoke about traveling. And though she expressed gratitude for her family and life in general, her eyes shone brightest when regaling her adventures abroad.

I started this book after my dad and Uncle Robert passed away. While writing this chapter, I called my Uncle Bruce because I felt as though I was writing about a stranger. I needed his insight. At one point, I asked, "Was your mom a happy woman?"

After thoughtful reflection, he replied, "I would say she was content." His hesitation and my own experience confirmed Erma's cloudy contentment.

Clouds of Introspection

I am blessed to have Erma's scrapbooks. Pouring through those in a pursuit to know her better, I found more clippings than photos. Erma read voraciously and collected thought-provoking poems, cartoon strips, and prose. I don't remember her ever sharing these nuggets of truth with me. Erma possessed a keen sense of humor, but I never heard her laugh out loud. She'd give a coy smile or maybe a chuckle but never a hearty laugh.

As I read the scraps she saved, I was surprised by what Erma kept. Her life didn't resonate with these tidbits of truth. We may agree with something, see its value, say we believe it—and not live it out. Erma's reflections produced little transformation. Erma failed to cross the bridge of truth. She remained trapped in her thoughts, stranded with her own opinion of herself. Her expectations snared her—her overthought and unreasonable expectations that neither she nor others could attain.

We can spend too much time thinking and too little disciplining our actions. As a follower of Christ who values Bible study, I don't want to peddle unlived truth. I want my introspection to produce confession, repentance, and character transformation. I long to live what I believe.

When I take an honest look at myself, I find I am more like Erma than I care to be. I enjoy travel. I collect poems, quotes, and cartoon strips. I'm also wired to depression and bent on introspection. How can I escape the endless trap of internal thoughts that lead me to fear and doubt? How do I build that bridge of action?

The Apostle Paul provides a blueprint. First, he tells us only twice to examine ourselves: once in 1 Corinthians 11:28, then again in 2 Corinthians 13:5. The first time, he instructs us to examine our hearts and confess any known sin. In the second passage, Paul calls us to evaluate our lives to see if we have been born again. Healthy self-examination consists of honestly asking myself, am I right with God? Do I have a real relationship with Him? Am I right with others? Once we make a clear assessment—with the Holy Spirit's help—we press on.

Healthy spiritual self-examination differs from the navel-gazing introspection that cripples us. Paul reminds us, "Let nothing be done through selfish ambition or conceit, but in lowliness of mind let each esteem others as better than himself. Let each of you look out not only for his own interests but also for the interests of others" (Philippians 2:3–4). I must choose to value others and their needs as much as I do my own. Erma's pride blinded her to the needs of others.

"Perfection is the enemy of good." This adage from the 17th century reveals the strife between achievable good and unattainable impeccability. The fruitless pursuit of the flawless agitates melancholy souls. Erma struggled with bouts of depression. I find some people suffer from depression, and others never do. The enemy at the root of it all is perfectionism, a wish-dream life that leaves us dissatisfied and even angry at reality.

Erma unintentionally chose a cloudy existence by choosing to look inward rather than out and up. My grandma Irène chose differently.

Irresistible Irène's Bright Beginning

Warning: Irène's story is difficult to read at times. Many of her experiences were... Sad. Hard. Ugly.

Two months *before* Erma's birth in the vast landscapes of Idaho, Irène Ricard entered the world in Nashua, New Hampshire, a bustling city famous for boot factories. On September 7, 1914, this baby girl sparked a ray of hope in her mamma's life. *A golden thread was born.*

"I will call her Irène, after my baby sister. Oh, I loved my little sister Irène! She died when she was two." declared Irène's mama, Rose Anna Ricard.

But Rose Anna's mother-in-law had a different idea. "You should name her Elis—after me. *I am* her father's mother."

The next day, Rose Anna—determined to name her daughter Irène—fled the confines of her postpartum convalescence to attend her baby's christening. In the early 1900s, postpartum recovery included a week of strict bed rest. It was unheard of for Catholic mothers to attend their child's christening; grandmothers brought the newborns to church. Rose Anna's audacity paid off.

Voila! The baptismal certificate reads Irène Ricard—no middle name. Rose Anna, as passionate as the language she spoke (French), made sure her baby girl would be called one name and one name only. Irène!

Irène's father, Dolphis Ricard, was determined to marry Rose Anna despite her mother's disapproval. He got Rose Anna pregnant out of wedlock. And just as he planned, Rose Anna's parents guarded her virtue with a shotgun wedding. Irène's folks exhibited the same tenacity as their French-Canadian ancestors. Hearty immigrants from Quebec migrated to New Hampshire and Maine. These sturdy souls took up fur trapping and lumberjacking.

Dolphis and Rose Anna conceived more than a daughter. They started a family living on a rollercoaster existence. Through multiple moves, Irène and her siblings were shuffled from one house to another like a deck of cards in her father's hands. With gambling debts, warrants for his arrest, and, for a time, bedridden with rheumatic fever, Irène's father failed to provide for his family. Despite his vices, he loved his children. My grandma shared fond memories of her daddy. She always spoke well of him. The crazy lifestyle that marked the first decade of Irène's life ended abruptly in 1925.

Dark Clouds Descend

I'll let Irène tell the next part of her story. Here's an excerpt from her memoir:

> "My father got an overland auto. He took us for our only fun trip ever to White City Park in Worcester, Massachusetts. We met a beautiful lady. She stopped and said to my dad, "Look," as she lifted a three-strand choker; She showed him a scar under the choker. She said, "I had a goiter like yours." (His was 18 inches around the neck. Mom had to make all his shirts because she could not buy any for such a neck.) The lady said, "I had surgery by specialists at the Deaconess Hospital in Boston. I'll take you there." Dad asked Mom if he should go. She said, "No, Nashua doctors said you'd die." Dad said, "Better dead than choke to death." Without her consent, he said "Goodbye" to all of us. During the operation, he had a heart attack. They revived him once. The second attack killed him. Relief told mom, "We don't pay to transport dead people; he'll be buried in a cemetery in Boston near the hospital." Proud Grandma Ricard paid to bring her son's body to Nashua, NH. She had the wake for him in her parlor. I had to bend over him to see his face above the casket. Without the goiter, it didn't look like him. Mom kept fainting all the time and ended up in the hospital.

My Grandma Ricard dyed all my pretty dresses in a boiler filled with black dye for mourning. My clothes came out all kinds of grays and blacks, even my socks and underwear. We were poor. So I wore black and gray clothes for years. To this day, I never wear black at funerals. I was almost eleven when he died."

A few months after subsisting on family charity, Rose Anna fell ill and had to be hospitalized. Her mother sought help from the church. The six children were placed in a Catholic orphanage. Irène spent the rest of her childhood there. Her only toys were brooms and scrub brushes. Playtime was minimal; work was constant. The state paid for the younger siblings, but Irène had to earn her keep (the national Fair Labor Act was not passed until 1938). She accepted her lot with cheerfulness. When her twin brothers saw her, they bragged to their friends, "That's Irène, our big sister!" The adoration of her little brothers brought her joy. Even in her late nineties, Irène grinned whenever she recalled this memory.

Each week, Rose Anna took her children to church. Then after service, they would go to relatives' homes for Sunday dinners. Irène's face lit up whenever she recounted the fun and laughter of a house full of aunts, uncles, and cousins playing cards and swapping jokes.

Irène excelled in math. After her eighth-grade graduation, she received a scholarship to go to business school. At the same time, the need for a full-time housekeeper at the orphanage came open. Staying meant she could continue to care for her younger siblings. Feeling a deep sense of family responsibility—Irène let the scholarship go. Nothing made Irène happier than being with family. She worked at the orphanage until she turned eighteen. Then another opportunity opened for her.

Irène received a job offer for housekeeping at a boarding house. It paid better than the orphanage, so she took it. Irène cleaned ten rooms and laundered and ironed shirts for sixteen men six days a week. She mended clothes, washed dishes, and did the spring cleaning for three dollars a week. Scandalous by today's standard, it was meager then, too. (In 1928, the average wage was approximately twenty dollars for a forty-hour workweek.)

Her First Love

Irène's love for people and sheltered upbringing in a Catholic orphanage produced a blinding naivety. One young man offended her scruples, attempting to French kiss her. She quit dating him. Soon after, Irène took up with a slick, young handyman, Arthur Manseau, from Biddeford, Maine. One hot summer afternoon Irène and her girlfriend took off to the far side of town to cool down at the local swimming hole. That's where her sunny smile caught Art's eye, and he captured her heart.

They married that fall, two months after Irène's nineteenth birthday. Poverty afforded them a simple ceremony, just a small church gathering. Irène married a virtual stranger. The longer they stayed together—the stranger it got.

Little Miss Sunshine Gets Burned

The newlyweds moved to Sanford, Maine, into Art's parent's house. Art often neglected his bride by barhopping with his buddies. One night when Art was out, Irène's drunken father-in-law attempted to rape her. She screamed, beating off his unwanted advances. Irène was three months pregnant at the time. The commotion woke her mother-in-law, who had gone to sleep in the backyard to escape his plastered pestilence. She flew into the room, yanking him away to protect Irène. After this, the newlyweds moved out.

Irène endured heart-wrenching labor to bring her firstborn into the world. The baby came breech. A neighbor helped administer ether, but the amount proved insufficient. Irène said, "I woke up screaming. It felt like they had pliers pulling my insides out."

The doctor called for more ether. The neighbor feared Irène would suffer an overdose. The doctor told Art to straddle his wife and crush the baby's head under her pelvis.

Arthur said, "The baby will die!"

"If you don't, your wife dies! The baby's head is stuck under her pelvic bone. The baby or your wife, which will it be?" the doctor retorted. By this time, the baby's neck had broken from the force of contractions. The neighbor tried to hide her horror and soothe Irène but to no avail.

In a drug-induced fog, Irène pleaded with her neighbor, "What's wrong?!"

In a sheepish tone, she replied, "The baby's dead."

Upon discovering it had been a girl, Irène reflected, "Thank God she'll never have to go through what I just did."

That night as my grandma lay in bed bleeding and swollen, her body and heart in agony, her husband abandoned her to medicate *his* misery. He returned home inebriated. Irène asked him to bring her a bedpan. "Get up and toilet yourself!" He slurred.

Later in life, Irène told me, "I should have left him then, but you didn't divorce a man for being a drunk in those days."

Irène had my mom, Claudette, a year later, then my uncle Joe eighteen months after Claudette. Arthur III, baby number three, arrived twenty months after Joe. Art neglected his family's needs throughout that time, forcing Irène to earn a living.

In times of desperation, Irène would go to the bar on payday and demand that Art hand over money to feed the kids, often resulting in violence. Art beat Irène. My mom remembers seeing her father chase her mother through the house with a knife.

The Sun Burns Back

In the summer of 1944, Irène filed for divorce. Art took her to the priest to attempt reconciliation. "Is she committing adultery?" the priest asked.

"NO! She's a good woman." Art protested.

"Then why is she trying to divorce you?"

"I drink," Art confessed.

"Nothing wrong with that unless you drink like a pig," the priest replied.

"Well, I do."

The priest turned to Irène, "If he takes a pledge to stop drinking, will you drop the divorce suit?"

"I would. Art's a good man when he's not drunk."

So, Art pledged to stop drinking, and everything seemed to be going well. Three months later, Irène conceived for the fifth time. One month after that, Art hit the bottle again. Soon he started hitting Irène again.

Some family skeletons need to stay in the closet. Such is the case with the incident that made Irène leave Art for good. She and her children moved in with her mother. I once heard that a Catholic priest told my grandmother to get a divorce. That's how notorious Art was.

After Irène left, Art stalked her, choking her at the restaurant where she worked. His sister Lea tried to beat him off with a broom, but he clenched Irène's throat until she passed out. A customer leaped from a booth to chase him down. Later, Irène had him arrested.

In court, the judge asked Irène, "Do you want me to put him in jail or order him out of the state?"

"If he goes to jail, my children will get teased at school about their father, the jailbird. Please, just send him out of state." The judge issued a restraining order forbidding him to be in Maine.

Irène's True Love

Irène began her new life as a single mother of four. Some things didn't change. She still worked long hours to feed and shelter her children. She managed to keep them one meager meal away from starvation. Sometimes that meal was onion soup with water for broth and day-old bread crusts for filler.

Irène's new singleness proved more peaceful. She no longer feared a violent drunk beating her or her children. During this time, Irène met Johnny Kerrigan from Galway, Ireland. Johnny knew Art and felt sorry for her. Johnny was a regular customer at the restaurant. They became very close.

Johnny would take Irène and her mother dancing and walk them home. He enjoyed Irène's children and took them on family outings. Johny wanted to marry her, but being a good Catholic son, Jonny honored his mother instead. He knew she would disapprove of him marrying a divorcée. My mom remembers Johny as a gentle and kind man. Her brothers liked him too, but he would be no more than a friend. Their friendship lasted fourteen years.

One day, Johnny's landlady called Irène, "Come quick! Johnny's very sick." This landlady had strict rules about no women in rooms, but this situation demanded an exception. Johnny had no family in America, and Irène was as close to family as Johnny had on this side of the pond. She went to his room and sat with him until the wee hours of the night.

"Why are you staring at me?" Irène asked

"You're so good and pretty. I can't take my eyes off you." His words took Irène by surprise. Irène saw herself as rather homely.

At 1:00 a.m., she tucked Johnny into bed and went home. At 5:00 a.m., the landlady called, "Irène, I'm so sorry, Johnny just died." Irène grieved the loss of her companion, but life went on.

Irène held many jobs over the years: housekeeping, waitressing, and working in a fabric mill. During WWII, Irène learned welding in an airplane factory. Welders earned good money, and factories loved little gals like her. She was small and could get into tight places in the plane that men had difficulty reaching. When the war ended, so did Irène's welding career. Soldiers returned to their civilian jobs, leaving many single moms unemployed.

After her three older children became adults and moved out, Irène moved to East Hartford, Connecticut. In East Hartford, she waited on tables at an Italian restaurant. Sometime after she started that job, her boss told her, "Irène, you should get a job at G. Foxes. Here the servers pool their tips, and you're getting shortchanged. You're very sweet. The customers like you. You make more tips than the other girls. You'd do better at Foxes; you could keep your tips there."

She thanked him and took his advice. She had no trouble getting hired at G. Foxes and worked there until she retired twenty-two years later. Shortly after starting at Foxes, she met her second husband.

Irène's Best Love

Fred Gayton worked retail. He supervised the women's department of Korvettes, one of the first discount department stores. Fred and Irène met in the spring of 1960 and married a year later, on June 23, 1961. I call Fred "Grandma's best love" because not only did he love and care for her, he *married* her. They enjoyed boating and having their families visit. Together they played with grandchildren, traveled, and enjoyed sunsets. Yet, the sun set too early in their relationship.

On Easter Sunday, 1967, Irène's son and his family came for Sunday dinner. Fred took ill, cutting the visit short. He went to the bedroom to lie down. I'll let Irène finish this story:

> "Freddie asked me to put my arms around him. "Oh my," he said, "the weight of your arms hurts." So, I lifted my arms enough for him to feel me but not to feel the weight of my arms.

> "Oh, my God!" he said. He sat up and fell back. I called the ambulance. He died by the time he got to the hospital."

Fredrick Gayton died of a heart attack, his arteries so blocked and hardened that the undertaker could not embalm him. Irène's "I do, . . . until death do us part" flew by in less than six years. Grandma didn't cry alone that day. Our whole family wept with her.

Her Last Love

Two months later, crazy with loneliness, Irène went on the rebound. She and a friend headed to the same club where she had met Freddie. Irène hoped to strike it lucky a second time out for a night of dancing. She did meet her third husband that night, but Lady Luck played a bad joke. Louis Kay ended up not being much better than her first husband. He verbally abused Irène and committed unspeakable atrocities. Irène kept her word and stayed committed to Lou for twenty-two years.

Hearing my grandma Irène's stories made me wonder: how could a woman who lived a life full of poverty and heartache keep a sunny disposition? Then it hit me—where I saw tragedies, Irène saw challenges. My grandmother never chose to be a victim. She mastered her circumstances by mastering her choices. No matter how dark the darkness was, Irène looked for the light. When hate raged against her, Irène crushed it with love. No matter what ugliness stared her down, she saw glimpses of redemptive beauty. Like a skilled hunter, Irène set her sights on the good in others and found it every time.

"I would ask you, dearest, to be very generous with him always, and very lenient on his faults when he is not by," said Dicken's character, Lucie Manette. Her sentiments express my grandma Irène's heart towards those we find repulsive. Let's choose to speak graciously of others.

When Irène's life proved difficult, she chose to keep living. Not a begrudging existence grumbling about how unfair life is, Irène believed life is good. Content to reap what she sowed, Irène never felt entitled to anything. Irène took responsibility—even for poor decisions. She didn't complain about the consequences or circumstances. Every morning, regardless of the weather, the sun rose in Irène's heart. And each day, she shined, living her life sunny side up.

Since Irène found happiness in a tragic life and saw good in sinful people, then one would think an easier life should produce greater enjoyment and appreciation of others, right? Yet, that's not what I observed.

No, doubt Erma and Irène came hardwired with different personalities. Each personality has strengths and weaknesses. Over time our characters—left unchecked—will get bigger but not necessarily better. The last decade of Erma's and Irène's lives illustrates this point. Let's take a look at how they finished.

Choice Meditations

1. Erma and Irène both worried at times. What worries you? Read Proverbs 12:25.

2. What does anxiety lead to, according to this verse?

3. Are you experiencing depression right now?

4. Can you think of a Scripture passage that assures you of God's care or His ability to resolve your problems? Use a concordance, find it, and make that your "good word" that can restore joy.

5. Read Proverbs 4:23 and Philippians 4:8–9.

6. How are heart-keeping and housekeeping similar?

7. What should we focus on in life?

8. What are some ways you saw Irène practice this truth?

9. How will you choose to practice this truth?

Choice Considerations

1. Do you tend to be a "glass half empty" or a "glass half full" person? Do you tend to endure life or enjoy life?

2. How grateful are you? Do you thank God daily for your day's blessings and trials?

3. In what positive ways have difficulties changed you?

4. How do you respond when you don't get what you feel is your due?

5. When people disappoint or mistreat you, do you still speak well of them (or at least choose not to tell others of their misdeeds)?

Choice Actions

1. Start your day and end your day with thanksgiving.

2. To rejoice is a choice. Start a joy journal. Each day write about something you've enjoyed. *Re*joicing recycles joy, reflecting on that which brought joy in the past. On days that seem joyless, reflect on past entries.

3. Go out of your way to help someone once a week.

4. Compliment someone every day.

5. When you feel angry or disappointed in someone, take a moment to reflect on their positive qualities instead of dwelling on their flaws.

6. When you do a job you don't like, think of one positive aspect of that job and thank God for it.

A Far, Far, Better Thing

The End of the Tale

Stand at the crossroads and look; ask for the ancient paths, ask where the good way is, and walk in it, and you will find rest for your souls.
Jeremiah 6:16

The new millennium ushered in not only a new era, but an unexpected reunion as my family relocated to Hillsboro, Oregon; the Gassers (my husband, four children, and I) arrived from Wisconsin in January 1999. Six months later, my parents came from Washington State. By early 2000, both my grandmothers sold their homes and moved to join us—Erma from California and Irène from Connecticut. I never dreamed I'd live so close to my parents again, let alone both of my grandmothers.

Things many families take for granted, like celebrating birthdays and holidays together, we began to enjoy for the first time. Now my folks and grandmas could attend my children's school programs. We enjoyed their concerts, plays, and sporting events *together*. The privilege of proximity allowed me the opportunity to know my grandmothers better. It also gave me a front-row seat for their last years.

At eighty-six-years old, both my grandmothers left their homes of fifty-plus years. Leaving familiar climates and surroundings, they said goodbye to the few friends their age still living. Moves are stressful for anyone, but can you imagine the challenge of moving to a new region when you're in your eighties? Consider this question carefully. God does not guarantee we get to stay in our homes all our lives. Will we choose to make a necessary transition, or will someone have to decide for us? Will we be willing or fight it tooth and nail? Both of my grandmothers made a *grand* choice. They chose to move near their children when they realized they could no longer keep up their homes, and their children lived too far away to help them.

My folks did not have to argue with them or talk them into it. They didn't have to drag them out kicking and screaming. My grandmothers didn't put up a stubborn resistance and make my parents worry about their safety or insist their children move by them. Both Irène and Erma knew the time had come and chose to move.

What a gracious gift they gave their children. Choosing to move where we can be cared for properly relieves our families of the burdens of worry and unpleasant confrontation. As I write this chapter, my mother, at a young seventy-nine, is downsizing and selling her home. She's chosen to move into a senior facility that offers independent living, assisted living, nursing, and memory loss care. She felt moving to be near my husband and me was not her best option since we may not stay here for another twenty years. Planning twenty years out for her is reasonable since her grandmother and mother lived to be a hundred. Her choosing to move now relieves me of concern for her safety. I'm thankful she followed her mother's and mother-in-law's example. I have friends who are not so blessed.

Their Last Chapter Begins

At first, the challenge of relocating seemed harder for Irène. Extroverts need people. Moving into a regular apartment complex filled with mostly young professionals gave her no opportunities to make friends. My mom tried to alleviate her situation by taking my four-year-old son for a weekly visit. Irène taught him card games and colored with him. She always had treats for him to eat. She'd toss her change in a piggy bank for him and send Jon home with the proceeds after showing him how to count it. They enjoyed those visits together, and I treasure Jon's opportunity to interact frequently with his great-grandma. However, it wasn't enough to fill Irène's longing for friendships. She became depressed.

About a year later, Irène relocated five miles away to a senior apartment building in North Plains. In a small community with lots of neighbors to get to know, she perked right up. Irène delivered meals on wheels until she broke her hip at ninety-eight. She volunteered at the senior center, washing dishes and setting tables. Finally, when she no longer had the strength or balance those tasks required, she became the official greeter. She loved giving hugs. For a few years, Irène put up the flag every morning and took it down every evening. She considered tending the flagpole a great honor. She walked a mile or two around town every day until she broke her hip. These walks provided the opportunity be get acquainted with many residents of North Plains. They all seemed to know my grandma Irène. There were never strangers in her life, only friends she hadn't met yet. She attended an exercise class for seniors until her last move to an adult foster care facility at one hundred years old.

Though both of my grandmothers exercised wisdom when it came time to make a final move, only one seemed to take full advantage of the new possibilities. One event during a family gathering illustrates it best. It happened after our second Thanksgiving meal together.

I had spent a lot of time and prayer preparing an activity for after the family feast. I wanted to facilitate a fun time of interaction between my mom, grandmas, and four children. Making gingerbread houses struck me as the perfect project, a sweet way to work together and prepare decorations for Christmas. I baked enough walls and roofs for four houses, one for my folks, one for each of my grandmothers to take home, and one for our house. Each of my kids paired up with a grandma, except Jenni. She got stuck with her mom, yours truly. It seemed to be going just as planned. I have pictures of everyone smiling. We licked frosted fingers and nibbled on candy, laughing and having a wonderful time. Then, when Anna and Grandma Erma finished basic construction and started decorating the outside of their house, Erma left the table. She went to the living room and sat in an easy chair.

Maybe she felt tired or bored. Maybe. Or maybe she didn't like working with a twelve-year-old. Maybe my daughter and Erma had different ideas about decorating. We will never know because she never excused herself or explained why she left the table. Later, when the projects were complete, we took pictures. Erma refused to come and have her photo taken with Anna. My mom felt so sorry for Anna. To top it off, when it came time to send the gingerbread house home with Erma, she flat-out refused the gift—the gift I had prayed about and spent so much time and money preparing—the gift she worked on with her great-granddaughter. My grandma rejected a present intended to bring Christmas cheer to her home.

"Oh, no, you take it home," she told me as I offered to take it to her car as she was leaving.

"But Grandma, we already have one," I explained again.

"Well, Anna can put it in her room. I'd rather not have it, thank you."

Ouch. I cannot judge Erma's motives. I've already shared a few speculations. I can tell you her actions and words put a damper on the day. We never made gingerbread houses together again. Oh, my kids and I did, and sometimes my mom and Grandma Irène joined us, but not Erma. It never became a Thanksgiving tradition.

On the other hand, Grandma Irène paired up with my youngest, seven-year-old Jon. She kept that gingerbread house displayed in her apartment year-round for several years and bragged about it to everyone. That's gratitude at its best!

Irène was the social butterfly; Erma was the wallflower. Erma's introverted personality made adapting to her new home easy. Our occasional family get-togethers and routine visits from my dad and uncle satisfied her relational needs. She found an opportunity to sew quilts for the fire department to give away to children displaced by house fires. She kept a brag book of her quilting. My dad would take pictures of her creations and help her put the pictures in her scrapbook. She made dozens of small quilts for the next six or seven years until mild dementia rendered her incapable of arranging the fabric in the correct patterns.

Though healthy for her age, Erma lived a sedentary lifestyle. Her lack of physical activity led to a rapid decline in her mental and physical fitness. Two years after moving to Oregon, she ended up in an assisted living facility. The assisted living center offered many group activities—day trips, game nights, and a quilting circle, to name a few. Erma chose *not* to participate in anything. She quilted alone in her apartment. She could see quite well and spent much of her time reading romance novels. I wonder if her choice of reading material contributed to her unreal expectations in life. I encouraged her to volunteer to read mail or the newspaper to someone in her building who couldn't see. She had no interest in the idea. Her sister, Alba, depended on the generosity of friends to read her mail to her. What a shame, Erma, with excellent eyesight, living amid many near-blind folks and unwilling to lend an eye.

Even though she appeared content with little to no social interaction, the lack of simulation allowed her brain to atrophy. Her lack of physical activity caused her to lose mobility, and she spent the last two years of her life in a chair or bed.

"Use it or lose it" is no trite saying. This hardcore reality bears swift witness against every area of life. God has given us everything––health, money, time, abilities––as stewardships. Like the foolish steward who buried his talent, God will take away what we don't use well. I saw this in my grandmothers' last years. Irène kept investing while Erma's abilities dwindled through neglect.

Irène and Erma had different tastes in décor. Both finished their days in one-bedroom apartments. Irène's was tidy and well organized but full of clutter that reflected what she loved: angels because she appreciated God's care for her; dolls because she adored children. The angels and dolls doubled as toys for young visitors. Family artwork hung on her walls, paintings done by both children and adults because she valued our creativity. The final elements of décor in Irène's home were photos. Lots, and lots of pictures because, more than anything else, Irène loved people.

Erma also decorated with things that reflected her heart (we all do). Her place was immaculate, uncluttered by tacky knick-knacks like Irène's. Erma's home resembled a 1950's Better Homes and Gardens photo. An Italian glass vase on a shelf, a cloisonné bowl from China on her coffee table, and her father's fine scroll carving of Psalm 23 hung over the couch. I don't recall any family pictures in the living room, a few in her bedroom, perhaps. She loved her travel and her collection of beautiful family heirlooms. She found contentment in a few occasional visitors, but Erma expected children to be quiet and touch nothing.

Appearances and Reality

Like Erma's heirlooms, the appearance of beauty can be fragile. In contrast, true beauty transcends appearances and remains sturdy against the falls and failures of life. Erma and Irène resembled their treasures, and like their treasure, they were both put out for display.

Erma found travel and possessions more interesting than people. She'd rather discover a new country than a new friend. Material things possessed more beauty than relationships, in her estimation. Her possessions were quite important to her. She painstakingly decided who would get what. Then she changed her mind, giving much of it away to a museum.

Before delivering the heirlooms to the museum, my dad decided to photograph my daughter modeling Erma's mother's dresses, including her wedding dress. Erma cringed, insisting, "These dresses are old and fragile. She'll ruin them!"

My dad retorted, "I will have pictures of my granddaughter in my grandmother's wedding dress as well as the others!" Thanks to my dad, our family enjoys those photos and the bridge they build between the five generations.

My father agreed to transport Erma and her treasures (her mother's dresses included) to the museum in Wells, Nevada. On the way down, they stopped at her sister, Lola's. After Erma had gone to bed, Lola and my mom went through the old trunk. Lola discovered her father's pocket watch, a retirement gift from the Union Pacific Railroad. "Doesn't Bob collect pocket watches?"

"I'm not sure," responded my mother.

"Well, I'm pretty sure he does. What is my sister thinking, giving Daddy's watch to a museum?! His grandson should have it! Here, give this to Bob, and *don't* tell Erma!"

Bob's aunt knew and cared about him more than his mother. Erma cared more about the world knowing her family than she cared to know them herself. Herein lies the source of her Eeyore disposition: one can love places and things, but places and things will not love you back. My husband is fond of reminding the congregations he serves, "There are only two things that last forever—the word of God and human souls. That is where we should invest." These are also the only two things that will profit us. "What does it profit a man if he gains the whole world and loses his own soul?" asked Jesus. The answer? Absolutely nothing! God can love us through His written word (the Bible) and the living Word (Christ). Other people can love us. When love flows in those directions, it becomes like the water cycle, endless and life-giving. When love is misplaced, it leaves a soul withered and dead. Let's choose *not* to love what can't love us back.

Erma won a seat on the Senior Rose court at Cornell Estates two years in a row. Her first year, she was elected as the Queen by her peers. This honor includes a special luncheon and ceremony given by Portland's Rosarians and a ride in the Rose Parade. To her neighbors at the senior assisted living facility, Erma's quiet aloofness gave her a lovely mystique. Erma was always dressed in a clean, classic manner and was a handsome woman. She looked the part of a Rose Queen, always polite and gracious, at least to strangers.

Erma's family knew a different woman. At times, Erma displayed the disdain of Marque Evrêmonde (the antagonist of *A Tale of Two Cities*) for those she considered beneath her class. In our eyes, ugly attitudes and comments marred Erma's appearance. Consider, for instance, her racist remarks. She noticed my daughter talking to a boy and assumed Rachel was dating the Hispanic fellow. Erma's derogatory comment hurt on two levels.

First, Rachel didn't have a boyfriend at the time. Second, we could not care less about what ethnicity people are. Racism is an ugly form of hatred! Love, on the other hand, embraces diversities.

Irène loved people. Like Dickens's Lucie Manette, Irène graced our families as "a golden thread." She, too, rode in parades. Almost every year she lived in North Plains, the Mayor asked her to join him in the Garlic festival parade. She waved and smiled at the neighbors she delighted in. She also rode through town on a motorcycle one year with a local motorcycle group that did a fundraiser for the senior center, thanks to Irène's encouragement. It all began with a compliment from a biker.

"Hey lady, I like your hat!" the burly man in black leathers called out to Irène.

"Then you should come to the senior center and buy one for your grandma! I make and sell them to help fund the place," Irène responded without missing a beat.

"I'll do that." And he did. That day, a friendship began that led to this man starting a fundraiser for the center. Irène's honest, friendly engagement with this man lead to raising thousands of dollars for the senior center in North Plains. Her hat was not elegant, nor was her appearance striking like Erma's, but her genuine care for people—all people, even rough-looking bikers— was a beautiful reality.

Now, I love both my grandmothers. I hope I have not glorified Irène too much. She was not perfect. She could be loud, anxious, and bordered on obnoxious at times. She had a temper and yelled—a genuine stress monster on occasion. I also hope I've not vilified Erma too much. She was well-mannered, soft-spoken, and an interesting conversationalist. These are both women I have benefitted from and, in diverse ways, admire. Yet, the contrasts between them are stark. I stated in the first chapter the importance of finishing well. To her credit, Erma did just that.

Their Last Chapter Ends

The day before Erma died, she spoke unusually kindly to her caregiver, my friend Evelyn. She thanked her for her care. Her comments seemed odd since her normal conversation tended towards criticism. She thanked my mom, her daughter-in-law of fifty years, for taking care of her finances and visiting her weekly. Then she said something that blew my mother away. "I love you, Janet." In all those years, Erma had never spoken those words to my mom. As my mom left, Evelyn pulled her aside. "Erma doesn't have much time left. I think she is making her peace. It will only be a day or two before she goes."

Evelyn has been caring for the elderly for over twenty-five years. She's watched lots of people die. She knew this behavior was indicative of one's last days. Sure enough, the next morning, the dawning of her ninety-seventh birthday, Erma Beatrice Donaldson got what she had wished for during the previous three years—the end of her life. I had a bouquet and was ready to walk down to Evelyn's to tell my grandma happy birthday when the phone rang.

I answered, "Hello?"

"Teri, this is Evelynn. Your grandma just passed away."

"I'll be right over," I assured her.

I walked down with the flowers and gave Evelyn the bouquet, thanking her for her caring service.

Evelyn Jones and I had been friends for about five years before Erma moved into her adult foster care. Our relationship flowed naturally from the friendship between our sons, who were classmates. I remember shortly after we met saying, "Both of my grandmas just moved to town. Don't be surprised if I call you to see if you have room someday."

My mom also got to know Evelyn. Her genuine care for her residents and the way she kept her home, plus the fact that she only lived two blocks from me, and a half-mile from my mom, made Evelyn's home the obvious choice when Erma and Irène needed around-the-clock care. What a blessing she has been to my family. I'm so glad God made us both neighbors and friends.

About a year after Erma died, Irène broke her hip. After a stay in the hospital, she needed nursing care for a couple of months. Of course, we called Evelyn, but her rooms were full. Evelyn gave up her guest room, her son's old bedroom, to squeeze Irène in. That was a hard stay for Irène, secluded in a room with little social stimulation. She determined she would heal and get back home, and she did.

However, being in her apartment failed to stop the ravages of age on Irène's body. When I'd visit, she updated me on her most current physical challenge, including her prolapsed rectum. Repair surgery for a younger person would be a snap; due to her age and heart condition, that option was off the table for Irène. After reporting on each of these painful challenges, she always said, "C'est la vie!" Her pleasant tone voiced her determination to keep enjoying life. Her French heritage remained a source of joy for Irène throughout her days.

Two years later, after her 100th birthday, it became apparent to my mom that Grandma could no longer care for herself. The daily visits by my mom and Irène's neighbors no longer sufficed. Irène reluctantly permitted my mom to call Evelyn again. "But I'm only going if Erma's old room is available, the one with the window that faces the street!"

Evelyn had already made a verbal agreement with someone else for that room. "But they haven't given me any money." Evelyn told my mom, "If you want it, it's yours. I love having Irène here!"

Irène moved for the last time. Unsure of this new arrangement, she kept questioning if it was necessary. We assured her it was, and after her friends began dropping by to visit, Irène settled into

Evelyn's home. She thanked Evelyn daily for cleaning her and helping her with toileting. Irène thanked her for the meals and for making her bed. Irène paid for every bit of it but never acted as if she deserved it. She expressed gratitude in the most humbling circumstances.

One month after moving, Irène Kay, at the age of one hundred years and six months, passed into eternity in the same bed as Erma. It was the fourth and final commonality between them. Only now, I couldn't just run down the street.

By this time, my husband and I had moved to Kansas. I had made a trip back to help her make this last move. She and I hugged each other more tightly than usual when I left. We both knew it might be our final goodbye. It was. I miss her deeply. I wept both tears of joy and sorrow as I wrote her story.

While researching for this project, I found an amusing book, *The Tale of Two Biddies,* by Vicki Kuyper. Ironically, hers was released at the same time I began writing mine. In it, she also describes her two grandmothers and what she discovered about aging from them. She nick-names them St. Katherine and the Dragon Lady. It's a fun read, and I do recommend it. Yet, as I expected, St. Katherine had a typical life, and the Dragon Lady lived a rather tragic one. Quite the opposite of what we observed in my grandmothers' lives.

Irène experienced overwhelming tragedy and trauma for much of her life. These painful experiences impacted her with grief. Yet, those feelings did not define her. Erma, on the other hand, lived an almost idyllic life. She, too, had painful losses, still not as extreme as Irène's. What caused Erma's character to be marred by a gloomy disposition while Irène warmed the world around her with cheer?

Quite simply, the direction they chose. Erma made choices based on an inward focus, and Irène focused on the world outside herself. One looked inward, the other up and out. One let her pride get the better of her, while the other humbled herself under the mighty hand of God.

Now that we know good circumstances don't guarantee good character, what characteristics do we want to develop? If we grow grand, it will happen because we depend on the *grand*ness of God to rewire our natural dispositions. As we move on in this pursuit, we'll discover appealing qualities in some of the well-aged women I remember, traits they developed by choosing an upward and outward focus.

". . .and I hear him tell the child my story, with a tender and a faltering voice.
"It is a far, far better thing that I do than I have ever done; it is a far, far better rest that I go to than I have ever known."
Charles Dickens, Tale of Two Cities

Choice Meditations

1. Carefully read Ecclesiastes 11:10–12:14. Get a good commentary if you have one. Why is making good choices today so important?

2. Read 2 Corinthians 12:9–10 and Psalm 73:26. In light of what you've discovered, write a personal prayer of commitment to living well in a worn-out body.

Choice Considerations

1. How is your body already experiencing decline?

2. Listen to yourself this week. Do you hear complaining, bitterness, or contention (expressing frustration with your circumstances)? Or do you voice contentment, gratitude, and hope?

3. Are you a good steward of your body (consider your eating habits, exercise, and sleep)?

4. Reflect on your grandmothers. What have they taught you? Thank God for those lessons.

Choice Actions

1. Based on your self-examination in question 3 above, choose one thing to do daily that would improve your health.

2. Now pick three more things and mark one on your calendar at three-month intervals. For example, say it's January. I'm going to start walking for ten minutes daily. April: I will begin eating one raw green thing every day. July: I will stop drinking caffeinated drinks afternoon each day. October: I will drink a glass of water half an hour before each meal. By doing this consistently, we can develop four new healthy habits of choosing in just a year!

3. Make a conscious effort to thank each person who serves you, like cashiers and receptionists.

4. Write a letter to each of your children conveying an important lesson you've learned. Compliment the traits you appreciate in them. Finally, express your love for them. You may choose to do this for your sons/daughters-in-law too.

PART 2

The Greats

Examples and impressions left by two of my great grandmothers
and two of my great aunts.

5

Sweet Sadie

Living in Loveliness

(My father's grandmother, Erma's mother)

The glory of Lebanon shall come to you: the cypress, the pine, and the box tree together,
To beautify the place of My sanctuary; and I will make the place of My feet glorious.
Isaiah 60:13

Thud! Suitcases hit the floor. My daughter, Rachel, continued telling us about all her adventures in France. At sixteen, she traveled further than her navy brat mom. We were happy to let her go and thrilled to have her *home*—safe and sound. Zzzzip! Already rifling through her bags, Rachel handed gifts to each family member.

"Here, Mom, these are for you!" she chirped, carefully sliding some sheets of paper from the front pocket of her carry-on. She gave me a big grin, "I got them for you at the gift shop in the Louvre. What do you think?"

What did I think? She had called me from the Louvre as she gazed at the original Mona Lisa. I was thinking then what I thought now, green thoughts of envy. Oh wait, she meant, what did I think of the prints. I looked at two familiar works of art by French impressionist Claude Monet, *Water Lilies*, and *Woman Facing Right with a Parasol.*

"I love them! Thank you so much! They're a wonderful pair. They match the blue wall perfectly!"

These pictures remind me of Rachel and how I prayed for her on that mission trip. The prints also illustrate my memories of Sadie Burton, my great-grandmother. You met her earlier. She's the mother of Alba, Lola, and Erma.

Much like a Monet, my memories of Sadie come in simple impressions: the white-haired woman sitting quietly under the verdant canopy of a shade tree or the well-aged woman standing in a yard wearing a freshly pressed, blue cotton dress, her spotless white apron flapping in the wind. As I ponder her, my mind floods with vague impressions that lack the defined details of reality. So, why write about this woman I barely knew—this woman seventy-seven years older than me? Because those memories, like a pebble dropped in a pond, rippled through my house. Her taste in décor became mine.

Pinterest replaced many home magazines, but at one time, women took pages out of magazines to save for future reference. Memories of Sadie's house inspired me like pages torn from *Better Homes and Gardens.* I live in a home surrounded by a style that was first hers. Objects that once filled her shelves now embellish my house. Sadie combined complex and simple elements, displaying a less cluttered Victorian flair. About a dozen years ago, my husband asked, "Does our living room need to be so feminine?" I took a thoughtful look around the room; off-white lace curtains, hues of blues melting into purples, and a ceiling border of Irises. That's when it dawned on me; I decorate like a grandma, not just any grandma. My living room reminded me of Great Grandma Burton's.

The Loveliness of Light

Light, full and bright, lavishes many of Claude Monet's paintings. This lovely element creates one of my most vital impressions of Sadie's home. Sitting at her table for a modest noon meal, I remember sunlight sparkling through the cut-glass tumblers and a crystal relish tray. The walls of that room, painted in the pale hue of jonquils, enhanced the sun rays streaming through the windows. Sadie tied every curtain back to welcome this warm guest into her home.

"Then God said, 'Let there be light'" (Genesis 1:3). With one short sentence—one breath—God illuminated everything. The making of light marks His first recorded, creative act. God's creation of light marks the calendar as the beginning of time itself. Its presence is essential to both time and life. We need light.

Sunlight provides our primary source of natural vitamin D, which most of us are not getting enough of. Our cancer-phobic, sun-screened, sunglass-wearing, indoor-dwelling culture deprives us of this vital nutrient, but Sadie's generation knew none of this folly. Born in the Victorian era, Sadie enjoyed the sunshine with bare arms, or at least half-bare arms, squinting eyes, and enough natural vitamin D to see her through ninety-nine years of living.

Undoubtedly, being born before indoor electricity gave Sadie a deep appreciation for a well-lit home. Why endure the smell of burning oil during the day if you don't have to? We take our switch flipping for granted, but natural light outshines the artificial. Plus, it's free!

Choose to Live in the Light

The house I hung those Monet prints in, the one with a blue wall, had a dark living room. The day I visited it with a realtor, every light must have been lit. I didn't notice because I focused on the size and layout of the place. Note to self: never buy a house until you see it with no lights on. Two small, north-facing windows exposed a backyard bordered by several Douglas firs. Clouds shroud the sun for most of nine months in the Pacific Northwest. Between the house's western Oregon location, tall trees, and north-facing windows, there was no way for the sun to shine into that house. When we replaced the roof a few years later, we popped a couple of holes in the living room ceiling and installed skylights. One of the best investments I have ever made!

Light affects our mood and productivity. Seasonal Affective Disorder (SAD) afflicts many residents in the Pacific Northwest. Ironically, the main symptom of SAD is seasonal depression. Doctors treat this condition with light therapy. A Swiss Federal Institute of Technology study suggests that indoor natural light increases productivity.

Besides being physically beneficial, light enhances our spiritual health by providing a picture of Who God is. The Bible spells it out clearly, "God is light and in Him is no darkness at all" (1 John 1:5). Jesus said, "I am the Light of the world. He who follows Me shall not walk in darkness, but have the light of life" (John 8:12). God exists as the epitome of grand. If we choose to be grand, we must first decide to walk in the light of the gospel of Christ. Otherwise, our souls will perish, and the profit of our endeavor to live well will end at the grave. So, how do we choose to walk in the light? By following Jesus, the way, the truth, and the life (John 14:6).

He made the way for our forgiveness by dying in our place on the cross. He revealed God's truth. Because of our sin, we stand condemned, but Jesus came to save us from that judgment (John 3:17). He rose from the dead on the third day as proof that God accepted His sacrifice on our behalf and gave us His everlasting life. To come out of spiritual darkness, I stopped going my way. That led me to death (Proverbs 14:12). I quit believing my truth. Since I am finite, my understanding is limited. At best, what I conceive in my mind as truth is a partial truth, a lie. Finally, I quit living my life for myself and began living in the resurrected power of Christ in me (Galatians 2:20), a life lived for others.

Let's choose to live in the Light of God's love and forgiveness and let His word be a lamp to our feet daily (Psalm 119:105). Choosing physical and spiritual light is essential in our pursuit of growing grand.

Remember the crystal relish tray I mentioned earlier? I think that's where my Pollyanna affection for crystal began. I love the scene in that old Disney movie with Haley Mills where she pulls back the dusty, old drapes in the grumpy widow's home. Suddenly the light refracts through the crystal fringe of a Tiffany lamp; the light shatters into hundreds of full-spectrum shards, tiny rainbows all over one wall. Pollyanna gets a brilliant idea and removes the crystals, then hangs them on strings across every window in the room. Like magic, sparkling splinters of rainbow color dance across the entire room, even the ceiling and floor. Light is the source of color. And color, like all of God's gifts, provides us with many benefits.

Impressions of Vibrant Color

The little white house sat on the road like a drawing in a young child's picture. Two simple four-pane windows hung on either side of the front door. The roof peaked above the door in the center of the small dwelling. Flowers of every color on the ground below the windows stood as doormen to greet Sadie's guests. My mother was no gardener, so we enjoyed plants left by the former owners. I loved the massive lilac bush and daffodils that colored my early spring days. Johnny Jump-ups grew randomly in the grass through the summer. I saw many purple and yellow blooms around my childhood home, but my great-grandma's yard glowed with every rainbow hue. Neon red geraniums stood behind hot pink, deep fuchsia, fiery orange, and dazzling yellow zinnias. A border of bright marigolds hemmed them all in. These colorful petals, like dapples of paint on Monet's canvas, left a mark on my impressionable young mind. Sadie's skillful use of color didn't end at her front door.

Inside Sadie's tiny home, throw pillows splashed color on her sofa. Several needlepoint creations accented the walls. Monet dappled paint on canvas; Sadie painted with thread. She dressed a young lad with multiple shades of blue, defining the folds and billows of his garments. He holds his large-brimmed, brown hat at his side. The fluffy white feather from his hat hangs just above the Kelly green ground. Kitty-corner from him hung his female counterpart, a young lady, her white dress billowing in the breeze. She wears a rose-colored bonnet; long pink ribbons float in the wind. A sash and the lass's lips are stitched in the same rosy tones. I remember these two of Sadie's needlepoint pieces best because I saw them often as an adult in my grandma's house long after Sadie passed away. The colors Sadie wove together continued to adorn walls in her absence.

Choose Color Intentionally

A well-done piece of art results from carefully placed color, whether a painting or needlepoint. It's no accident; the sky is blue, and the grass and trees are green. It was no accident that the tabernacle was crimson, blue, and purple. God chooses color intentionally, and so should we. I marvel at the sight of deciduous trees in the fall as the leaves take on glowing shades of crimson, burgundy, neon orange, and yellow. Did you know that orange makes us hungry and red flares a warning? Is it any wonder God chose to turn foliage into those colors in northern regions with long cold winters? "Hurry!" the autumn leaves shout. "Gather the harvest. Winter comes quickly!" their bright colors warn us.

Why might police uniforms be blue? Blue communicates justice and security. It represents divinity in the tabernacle because God is the ultimate source of justice and security. We look up at a blue sky. It reminds us of God's presence over us. Why are most landscapes bathed in green? Green is the most soothing color to the eye. It calms us. God designed the earth to make us feel at home—relaxed. The book of Revelation reveals God's throne of grace encircled in a rainbow that appears like an emerald (Revelation 4:3). He made Himself approachable. He calls us to Himself that we may find our home in Him.

What moods do we want our homes to reflect? If we desire harmony in our homes, do the colors we choose harmonize, or do they clash, stimulating emotional dissidence? How about gifts we give? Are we intentional in choosing colors the recipient will appreciate?

Author Carol Kent tells about a time she found herself floundering in despair. During her horrible trial, her sisters bought her a large bouquet of bright yellow roses with a note that read, "Dear Carol, you once gave us some decorating advice. You told us that yellow flowers would brighten any room. We thought you needed a little yellow in your life right now. Love, Bonnie, and Joy." That was choosing color intentionally! I have met both Carol and Bonnie. I've never had the privilege of meeting Joy, but I would describe those sisters as women who are growing grand. They are all grandmothers now. Many of the choices we'll consider in this book are the choices they have made. Choosing color intentionally is just one small choice, but what a powerful choice it can be.

Light and color serve as two elements of a lovely setting. The third element, design, acts as the director. Design takes hold of light and hue, giving them shape and purpose. It defines space in lines and contours. In Sadie's home, I saw intentional design in so many things.

The Loveliness of Intricacy

"Look, Mommy! She has a clock like ours." By age three, I'd visited many homes and gone with my mom to several stores, but I had never seen our clock anywhere else.

"Yes," my mom replied. "Her husband, your great-grandpa, made both of them. She has one, and we have the other."

Some people enjoy grandfather clocks. I grew up with a great-grandfather clock. Sadie's husband had taken up scroll carving after he retired from ranching. The craft of scroll carving seems obsolete these days. Today, similar work is done by laser. A discerning eye can tell the difference. Scroll-carved edges tend to be less smooth and retain the wood's natural color, while laser-cut pieces have precise edges burnished in black. The clocks of which I speak stand three feet tall. Various small pieces of wood, delicately carved, form an elegant cathedral. If I had a quarter for every time I heard someone say, "What a beautiful clock!" I'd be a wealthy woman. Oh, wait, I am a rich woman. This priceless heirloom keeps time in my home now.

Once the fascination with the twin clocks faded, I looked around Sadie's house for the first time. Not only had my great-grandpa made two clocks, but his hand-made occasional tables, corner cabinets, and letter holders filled Sadie's home. Her handiwork of needlepoint and crocheted thread doilies complimented the scroll-carved furniture. Like a can-can slip filling out a skirt, layers of intricate wood and thread lace held her home up in a timeless fashion. Yet, the complexity of these items was not overwhelming. The small rooms in Sadie's house felt spacious and uncluttered, harmonious with elaborate detail and ample margin.

Sadie's home, warm with light, alive with color, and engaging with design, always felt inviting. Whether I was three or thirteen, I enjoyed sitting in her house and admiring the lovely space she had created.

Choose to Cultivate Creativity

"Come with me, Dear," Sadie said as she put her hand gently on my shoulder, "and bring your dolls." I was eight years old, and she knew I would soon tire of the adult conversation in the living room. She ushered me into her bedroom and carefully took down the doll furniture that decorated her dresser.

"I think you are old enough to play with these. Now, this furniture is fragile. Will you be careful with it?"

I assured her I would. So, she left me to play with my dolls and her furniture. Then she returned to visit with her guests in the living room. Sadie treasured the scroll-sawed doll furniture crafted by her beloved husband. Sadie didn't have to risk sharing it. She could have just expected me to sit patiently with the grown-ups, but instead, she invited me to use my imagination and have space alone for some creative playtime. Sadie not only lived creatively, but she also cultivated creativity in others.

I remember one visit to her home in my teen years. I sat on her couch, drawing while the adults conversed. She came and sat by me, watching my strokes. When I paused, she asked to see my other sketches in the pad. Her interest and comments encouraged me and drew me into actually visiting with her. There I sat surrounded by displays of artwork she, her husband, her daughters, and even a few things her grandchildren had made, as Sadie encouraged me, the next generation, to continue to be creative. I'm embracing her legacy by encouraging the creativity I see in others.

My granddaughter now plays with that doll furniture. I added a couple of small porcelain dolls to the arrangement. She quietly whiles away the time as her younger siblings nap. I also stock plenty of crayons and paper for young visitors to enjoy.

The Tension between Creative Clutter and Obsessive Order

Lovely surroundings require order and cleanliness. Creativity often results in a mess. Think of all the lint that flew around Sadie's home as she and her girls cut quilt squares. Can you see her table strewn with thin wood panels as her husband laid out patterns to saw? Imagine the sawdust-covered workshop he spent so much time in. I remember the oil paint stains on my middle daughter's comforter from her artistic endeavors. I also remember noise: tap dancing shoes on my hardwood floors, piano scales, and the dissonance of miss-struck chords. Some of you may have been subject to squeaking violins or loud, awkward trumpet blasts. None of these sounds are conducive to a tranquil environment, but the fruit of these intruders adds great beauty to our homes and families as skills develop. Somehow, order is born from chaos and beauty from messes. To prize a clean, beautiful home too much robs our families of space to create. A homemaker obsessed with a clean house can be oblivious to the invisible eggshells her family navigates.

On the other hand, a neglectful housekeeper strangles creativity in clutter and filth. How can one make anything when flat surfaces lie buried and necessary materials hide in random places? This tension of finding the right balance of cleanliness and order versus creativity and mess eludes me. I ebb and flow through periods of productive messiness and a clean house. Maybe not obsessing about either is the key—like a day at the beach—enjoy the ebb and flow! After all, isn't that how God operates? He created from chaos a well-ordered world. Then He allowed it to fall into chaos again and, even now, is in the process of redeeming it. There will be a new heaven and a new earth. Someday my longing to dwell in a perfectly kept home will be realized, but not on this side of glory.

I think sweet Sadie had come to terms with that tension in allowing me to play with her doll furniture and being willing to let it go if it broke. Living in loveliness requires cling-free living—not clinging to things. Instead, we value people. People God created to be creative.

Sadie's doll furniture sits on my library shelves, acting as a home for a few porcelain dolls. These pretty toys remind me—houses are for people, for *fellowship*. A beautiful house doesn't guarantee a lovely home. Love makes it lovely; peace makes it pleasant.

I'm often alone in my empty nest. Yet, I still have dirty dishes. I still make messes while I create things. There will always be dust and dirt sneaking into my clean little house. Living in loveliness requires an ebb and flow between cleaning and creating with a gentle, peaceful attitude.

Choose to Have a Gentle, Quiet Spirit

A grand woman, in God's eyes, doesn't just look good. She *is* good, good in the sense that she trusts Him fully. Through faith, He gentles her. "Do not let your adornment be merely outward," God tells His daughters. "Rather let it be the hidden person of the heart, with the incorruptible beauty of a gentle and quiet spirit, which is very precious in the sight of God" (1 Peter 3:3–4). Early in my walk with Christ, this verse vexed me. I am not a quiet person. How can I ever be beautiful in God's sight? My voice booms at times. I laugh out loud and scream in pain. I can't begin to express my relief when I first discovered Peter was not talking about volume. It's not a quiet voice God's after. It's a quiet *soul*. He desires a soul unhurried, without anxiety, unflappable in trials, a soul at peace with circumstances and with Him.

It's tough, Sisters. I confess I am too often a stress monster. When my circumstances or the state of my house are out of control, Teri the troll tries to yell them into order. My fleshly resort to clamor (which, by the way, I know, is a sin) always fails. When I bark out orders in frustration, I get minimal compliance. My harsh tone stirs up strife and provokes resentment from those I love most. *Yikes!* How can those of us plagued with intense, anxious spirits be gentled? James reminds us that our tongues are a fire, a world of iniquity (James 3:6). What would you do if your body were on fire?

You remember the adage: stop, drop, and roll. With a slight adjustment, these instructions rescue me from my Mr. Hyde. I stop, drop, and pray when I feel my gut twisting with stress or hear my tongue turn into a flame thrower. I *stop* what I'm doing or saying. I *drop* to my knees and run to God's throne of grace (figuratively speaking). Then I *pray*, asking for His mercy in my time of need (Hebrews 4:16). He is the One thing I need most in those moments. I don't have the power to control my tongue or my circumstances, but God *does*. And He's there waiting for me to ask.

The prettiness of youth is fleeting. Years of gravity and depravity take their toll. We can all maintain our hygiene and wardrobes to be outwardly attractive, but the splendor of grand women emanates from within. Will others see in us the glorious, unfading beauty of a tender heart at rest that distracts them from our sunspots and wrinkles? If we fail to cultivate gentleness today, we won't have it tomorrow.

I asked my uncle, Bruce Donaldson, about his impressions of Sadie. He told me a story that confirmed my opinion of her.

"I remember during one visit with her, a thieving gypsy came to her door offering her a great deal on sealing her driveway. I could tell this guy was trying to con her, and she could feel it too. Grandpa had been dead for at least a couple of years by now, but without hesitation, she said, 'I'll have to talk to my husband about that. I don't make those decisions alone. Thank you for coming by.' I thought it was a very gracious way to deal with a thief."

Did you notice the mild manner Sadie used? My uncle heard no worry in her voice, just a calm, gracious response. He never heard her malign the man or complain of this solicitation. I sensed the same gentleness when she invited me to play with the doll furniture. I never felt I had to walk on eggshells around her. Erma's description of the young woman churning butter, complaining about all she gave up, was not the woman I knew.

At some point, Sadie experienced a metamorphosis. By turning her gaze from loss to gain, valuing what she had over what she lost, Sadie floated above discouragement. I never heard her complain.

I saw in her true contentment. Sadie displayed the imperishable loveliness of a gentle, quiet spirit.

Her example gives us hope. We, too, can grow grand. We need not feel victimized by our sin and suffering. To grow grand like Sadie, we need to choose to live in the light and choose color intentionally. We must choose to cultivate creativity in ourselves and others, but most of all, we need to develop the permanent charm of a gentle, peaceful soul.

Choice Meditations

1. Read Genesis 1:3–4 and Ecclesiastes 11:7. What do you learn about the nature of light?

2. In Psalm 119:105, 130, light is used as a metaphor for God's word. What similarities do light and the Bible share?

3. In Philippians 2:14–16, what action must we take to choose to be light?

4. Take some time to meditate on Genesis 1. Now go outside, or sit by a window, and simply enjoy the colors and designs you see around you. Be unrushed, unhurried. Relax. Choose to rest with a quiet spirit.

Choice Considerations

1. Are you starting your day by looking into the light of God's

Word?

2. How have you brought light to someone's life recently?

3. Do you enjoy the way you've decorated your home? How do others living there feel about the décor?

4. How are you and others you live with creative? Does your home provide a place to exercise that creativity?

5. Are you more of a Mary or Martha? Do you handle stress well, or is anxiety, like Dr. Frankenstein, transforming you into a stress monster?

Choice Actions

1. If the surroundings in your home do not bless you, pick one thing you can change to make it a more attractive place.

2. Take a light bath. Go outside on a sunny warm day. Take your Bible, read a favorite passage, and just enjoy the light, or sit by a sunny window if it's too cold. Cats know how to appreciate this kind of cleansing rest.

3. Make a list of your spouse, children, and closest friends. Now try to remember their favorite colors and jot those down. Keep that list in your purse when you shop for cards and gifts.

4. Mark time on your calendar this month to do something creative just for the joy of it.

5. Listen to your own words. Are they harsh or gentle? If we're using a harsh tone, it's because we're anxious or angry. And we need to stop and focus on the One thing that can quiet our spirits. Remember, when anxiety sets our tongues and actions on fire with harshness, we must *stop*, *drop*, and *pray*!

6

Resilient Rose
Anna

Living with Tough Stuff

(My mother's grandmother, Irène's mother)

My brethren, count it all joy when you fall into various trials, knowing that the testing of your faith produces patience. But let patience have its perfect work, that you may be perfect and complete, lacking nothing.
James 1:2–4

"You have a grandma?" I grappled with this new idea. At five, I believed only children had grandmas.

"Of course, I have a grandma," my mother replied. "And today, we're going to go visit her."

We stepped out of the car into the sunshine. A small, round woman with grey hair stood on the lawn. Her face lit up with joy as we approached. An exchange of French pleasantries rolled from their tongues as she and my mom embraced. Then my mother turned to me and introduced me to Mémère Ricard. Mom and Mémère continued speaking in their strange language. Hearing so much French confused me. I had listened to my mom and grandmother speak it occasionally, but mostly they spoke English. Now I felt like a foreigner among my kinfolk. With a broad smile on her face, my great-grandmother lowered her gaze. Her eyes met mine. Then Mémère reached out in a language I understood, a *hug*. Her soft arms drew me in. I found myself engulfed in the warmth of her plump figure. Then she led us into her house.

We walked through the front room straight into the kitchen. My mom and I took a seat at the table.

"Mémère is going to make us crêpes!" My mom's excitement made my mouth water. All my short life, whenever my mom made pancakes, she would sing the praises of the crêpes made by this mysterious woman.

"Mommy, these pancakes are yummy," I'd tell her.

"Oh no, these are far too fat and not crispy enough. Mémère's crêpes are so thin you can almost see through them. They're so crisp and tender. They melt in your mouth." Mom's eyes would drift, and she'd lick her lips. Now, I would finally taste the legendary treats.

Mémère took out a large bowl and collected various ingredients from the cupboard and fridge: flour, salt, and eggs. She beat them together, flipped the gas burner on, and pulled the cast iron pan onto the flame. She plopped a small lump of grease into the pan. It melted and soon began to sizzle. The aroma of bacon filled the little kitchen. With skill and precision, Rose Anna poured the thin batter onto the skillet and then picked up the pan, gently rolling it to spread the batter evenly. She flipped the crêpe with ease. Once done, she slid the crêpe out of the skillet and poured the next. In her hand, the pan became a conveyor belt of French delicacies. Her motion mesmerized me. My mouth watered.

Finally, Rose Anna joined us at the table with the plate of crêpes. My mom took a fork and lifted a golden marvel onto my plate. I poured maple syrup onto it and took my first bite. I still remember the thrill, the sensation of pure delight dancing on my taste buds, and the delicate texture between my teeth. This sweet introduction to Rose Anna left quite an impression.

As time passed, I discovered more and more about my mémère, Rose Anna Ricard. Crêpes serve as a metaphor for her life. She faced flaming trials that developed a cast-iron resolve in her will and solidified a delicious resilience in her soul. Her first encounter with grief came early. Her younger sister died at the age of two; Rose Anna was only four. Then her father passed away before she turned ten. Losing loved ones at such a young age taught Rose Anna to hold on to her memories and treasure time spent with those she loved. She enjoyed recalling how she cared for her baby sister, Irène. (Remember, in chapter two, I mentioned Rose Anna honored her sister's memory by naming her first daughter Irène.)

Rose Anna's childhood foreshadowed her life as a young wife and mother. Just as her father died when she was only nine, her husband died when her daughter, Irène, was ten. By the time Rose Anna turned thirty, her husband's death had condemned her to widowhood *and* an empty nest. This circumstance forced Rose Anna to place her children in an orphanage because she could no longer provide for them. I can't imagine the torture of this decision. Indeed, memories of being separated from her mother haunted her. After her father's death, she and her younger siblings were sent to Canada to live with an aunt and uncle.

In her nineties, Rose Anna recounted to me the cruelty of her stingy aunt. The woman practically starved the Ricard children. This aunt, who had agreed to care for them, would lock them in the attic, forcing the siblings to be quiet when they were not in school. Instead of going to school, young Rose Anna sought refuge in the home of a kindly neighbor. This woman pitied Rose Anna and fed her. She spent her days helping this woman in the yard and kitchen. As a result, Rose Anna missed much of her traditional education. She never learned to read but became a wonderful gardener and cook. My mother told me, "Memérè's roses grew the size of Jackie's face" (Jackie was my mom's little sister). Eighty years later, Rose Anna still praised the neighbor who sheltered her. She expressed genuine gratitude for that woman.

When Rose Anna's mother discovered her sister's neglect of the children, she moved them back to New Hampshire and placed them in an orphanage. Later, as a young widow, Rose Anna's children would go to an orphanage as she had. Life went on. And so did Rose Anna.

Choosing to Balance Sorrow with Joy

With a matter-of-fact tone, in broken English, Rose Anna shared her recollections with me. Her voice lulled me with an engaging rhythm. Sorrow and joy, winning and losing, life and death all ebbed and flowed through her stories, just as they run through ours. Choosing not to get stuck in either ditch moves us forward. Resilience travels the road between life's highs and lows. To grow resilient, we must let past joy carry us through pain and live out the lessons learned through trials. In the dark of night, we must choose to remember the sun will shine again. None of us experience all good or all bad in life. The key to resilience lies in a realistic, balanced perspective. Jesus displays resilience.

"Therefore . . . let us run with endurance the race set before us, looking unto Jesus, . . . who for the joy that was set before Him endured the cross despising the shame and has sat down at the right hand of the throne of God" (Hebrews 12:1 – 2). The wisest man to ever live, King Solomon, penned a whole book on mastering this balance. Ecclesiastes 3:1 sums it up best, "To everything, there is a season, (Remember, seasons change!), "a time for every purpose under heaven."

Expecting and the Unexpected

Rose Anna told me she and Dolphis Ricard w ere very much in love, but her mother *forbade* them to marry. Despite her mother's disapproval, Dolphis was determined to make Rose Anna his wife.

"I know a way she'll have to let us get married," he told Rose Anna. She naively joined in his conspiracy, clueless about how his forceful, physical contact would gain their nuptials.

Young Rose Anna, just eighteen-years-old, soon discovered she was expecting. Her pregnancy confused her. "How can I have a baby when I'm not married?" she pleaded with her mother.

Her mother questioned her and explained she had fornicated. Poor Rose Anna continued in ignorance, "How will the baby come out?"

"The same way it went in!" her mother retorted harshly.

Dolphis's plan worked just as he hoped. The two soon wed.

I've already told you about the birth of Rose Anna's first baby, Irène. Two years later came a boy, then another boy three years later. Rose Anna's fourth pregnancy delivered an unexpected outcome.

Rose Anna labored hard and long. She had birthed three children already, so she couldn't imagine why this delivery felt so excruciating. Finally, relief! The head was out. Soon the rest of the baby slipped into the midwife's hands. Instead of smiling, she gasped in horror.

Another woman, there to help, exclaimed, "It's a monster!" They thought it was a two-headed baby (conjoined twins). The midwife began unwinding the umbilical cord. With the bundle untangled, everyone sighed in relief. Two separate babies! However, the babies' heads crowned and came out together; each infant weighed a good six or seven pounds. Without anesthesia, Rose Anna birthed two babies at once and *lived* to tell the tale.

Today—when expecting mothers get to know the gender of the child before it's born—it's hard to imagine a time when you couldn't even be sure if you were having twins. Rose Anna started in labor expecting one big, healthy baby and ended up with two.

Rose Anna faced many other unexpected circumstances in her life. One, in particular, shaped my conviction against gambling. Rose Anna saved enough money for a down payment on a house; she earned this money, *not* Dolphis. And accumulating that down payment was no small feat since Dolphis gambled compulsively. But the bank refused to issue the title in her name, so, *legally*, Dolphis owned the property. One day, a knock at her door turned her world upside down.

"Mrs. Ricard?" the gentleman inquired.

"Yes."

"You're going to have to move out. I beat your husband in a card game, and the house is mine."

Standing on her doorstep, the stranger presented her with the deed to her house, only her husband's name was no longer on it.

"But I bought this house!" Rose Anna protested, "It's mine. I earned the money to pay for it. Not him!"

"His name was on the deed. Now mine is. It's my house," the man declared in a sorry, not sorry fashion.

I don't know how quickly she moved or where she ended up living. I do know she held no grudge against either of the men, and she was quick to share what she appreciated about her husband. "He loved his children. He'd play with them and talk with them. He was so kind to everyone. He had many friends."

Choose to be Flexible

"Take me out to the Ballgame. Take me out with the crowd," Rose Anna sang in her flat, less-than-melodic voice. It was her favorite song. She loved sports. Baseball, football, boxing, you name it, Rose Anna watched it. She enjoyed the action, the competition, and most of all, the anticipation of the outcome. Life often throws us curve balls and punches. No matter how much we plan and prepare, what we expect and get are often two different things.

Through Rose Anna's first, unexpected pregnancy, the surprise of the twins, and losing her house, we see the importance of being flexible. Teams and coaches have to make readjustments. Players get injured; opposing teams play better than expected. Like Solomon tells us, "The race is not to the swift, nor the battle to the strong . . . But time and chance happen to them all" (Ecclesiastes 9:11). If I want the grand characteristic of resilience, I can't let the unexpected disappointment and difficulties of life knock me off my game. I need to bend under the weight of these intruders, *without breaking*, and bounce back when trials subside. I must let go of my expectations and change up my game plan. Bitterness makes us brittle, hopelessness leaves us helpless, but flexibility frees us to rebound. And rebounding provides momentum to move forward in life—to keep on living.

This past weekend, I spent a lot of time making a fancy jello salad in a snowflake mold. I carefully layered various shades of blueberry gelatin mixed with cream, then fruit. I outlined the details with whip cream. It looked quite festive, but on our way to the holiday gathering, one sharp turn in the car sent it sliding off the plate. When I arrived and opened the hatchback to retrieve it, I found half of it on my car floor. *Eeew!*

Much to my husband's pleasure, I nonchalantly slid the good half to the center of the plate. My husband felt a bit sorry for me because of the effort that seemed wasted, but the truth is I did it for the sheer pleasure of being creative—*not* to impress anyone. I enjoyed seeing the finished product, and so did he; in the end, our audience of two was enough. When I put it on the table, I simply said, "I got hungry on the way over." After enjoying the laugh and telling the true story, everyone loaded their plates with the potluck offerings, even my broken salad. It proved to be a delicious dinner. I'm so thankful I didn't choose to spoil it with a sour attitude.

I know a jello salad is a small thing, but practicing with the lightweight disappointments will prepare us for the heavyweight hurts. Much like Rose Anna's two-headed "monster," horrible things don't always end up as bad as we think. On the other hand, like the house she could never return to, and her husband, who died at thirty-five, some negative things *are* permanent, but sorrow doesn't have to be.

Breaking Bad

Industry marked Rose Anna's character. Just like she labored to deliver twins two heads at once, she worked hard at every job. She considered no honest labor too demeaning, and even not-so-honest work was better than no work. She resorted to bootlegging to provide food on her table for a short time.

Prohibition had just started, and the Ricard household needed more income. Dolphis hatched a plan. He convinced Rose Anna to distill clear liquor, and then he'd invite friends over to gamble. He'd drink water while boozing his guests. Taking advantage of their drunken state, Dolphis won every hand. The plan worked well until the Feds showed up. They hauled Dolphis off to jail, leaving Rose Anna to care for her family alone. Fortunately, Dolphis charmed people in high places. His friend, the county judge, agreed to throw the case out of court, providing the Ricards quit their moonshine business. Soon after this, Dolphis died.

Once Rose Anna recovered from the shock, she found a job as a live-in caregiver for a tuberculosis patient. Later in life, she owned a restaurant—thanks to the cooking skills she learned as a child. Folks loved her cooking, and she loved to cook. My mom raved about the pies Mémère baked. Eventually, the restaurant closed. Rose Anna moved on.

My mom lived with her one summer. The two of them cleaned hotel rooms together. My mom was too young to earn a wage, so the owner paid Rose Anna, then Rose Anna would split it with her. Rose Anna's initiative and humility in finding work never went unrewarded. There comes a time in the lives of those who live long enough that working is no longer an option. When she could no longer care for herself, Rose Anna relied on her children. Those who could care for her were quick to honor the mother who had loved them as best she could through the trials of life.

One of Rose Anna's most remarkable acts of humility and initiative happened while living with her daughter Irène. The mother and daughter, ages 90-something and 70-something, struggled to make their life together work. Irène gave up her bedroom on the ground floor and slept upstairs because age rendered Rose Anna blind. Irène got very little sleep, traveling up and down to help her mother with toileting through the night. This routine played havoc with Irène's already high blood pressure. On top of that, Rose Anna had been blind for about a decade, resulting in Non-24, a blindness sleep disorder. Like an infant who has days and nights confused, Rose Anna had lost her sense of time.

Rose Anna's meager finances allotted her a social worker who dropped by once a month. During one of these visits, Rose Anna boldly requested, "You need to find me a nursing home. I don't want to kill my daughter. She can't keep taking care of me. It's too much for her! I don't want her to die before I do; if she does, I don't want it to be my fault."

Irène and the social worker began searching for Rose Anna's last home. They placed her at St. Elizabeth's—a top-notch Catholic nursing home just a short drive from Irène's house. Irène visited her mom *every* day.

Soon Irène began volunteering there. She'd deliver mail and run a weekly bingo game. Instead of draining her daughter's health, Rose Anna's choice *improved* it. Irène began to lose weight, and her blood pressure dropped. Rose Anna put her daughter's needs before her own. She learned long ago—life was not about her. At an age when some people start to feel entitled, Rose Anna rejected that temptation and did what was best for her daughter. She humbly took the initiative to leave a private home and institutionalize herself. Rose Anna did that hard job so Irène wouldn't have to.

❧ ⟶ ✿ ⟵ ❧

Choose to be Industrious

As American children, school teachers indoctrinate us with our "*inalienable rights*: the right to life, liberty, and the pursuit of happiness." We learned our world *revolves* around us, that pursuing happiness—our *individual* happiness—is our birthright. Is it any wonder that we've become a nation of entitled narcissists? A couple of years after I became a Christian, I read Roy Hession's book *The Calvary Road*, and he turned my false notions upside down.

> "And Jesus was willing to become that just for us—a worm and no man...that is what He saw us to be, worms having forfeited all rights by our sin, except to deserve hell."

"But dying to self is not a thing we do once for all. . .
All-day long the choice will be before us in a thousand
ways . . .It will mean a constant yielding to those
around us, for our yieldedness to God is measured by
our yieldedness to men."

God displays the grandeur of His character through Christ. "We
love him because He first loved us" (1 John 4:19). He took the
initiative to love. "For He made Him who knew no sin to be sin
for us, that we might become the righteousness of God in Him" (2
Corinthians 5:21). Jesus served His servants. The Good Shepherd
became our sacrificial lamb. The Lord of life died our death. The
King of glory left His throne to seat us in Heavenly places. In
light of this reality, those of us who follow Him kid ourselves if
we think any task is beneath us or that we should look out only
for ourselves. Grand women know the secret of joy, like the old
children's song, is Jesus, Others, put Yourself last and spell *joy*.

I remember preaching this sermon to myself as I cleaned the
bathrooms at Meadowood Baptist Church, the first church my
husband pastored. We were young, and the congregation very
small, but through the generosity of its founding members, we
enjoyed a nice size building. That building needed cleaning each
week. This small community of young couples and retired folks
had more time than money. Unable to hire a janitor, we agreed
to a cleaning rotation. It would be my family's turn to clean every
few weeks. I remember telling myself, "If I think I'm too good, as
a pastor's wife, to clean toilets, then I'm not truly good at all."

Since Jesus snatched me out of a cesspool of sin, I can scrub
toilets and wipe baby bottoms in the church nursery for His
glory. There is no service lowlier than the work Christ did for us.
"He became sin Who knew no sin" (lyrics from *Jesus Messiah*, a
principle from 2 Corinthians 5:21). We will never be as humbled as

He was or go as low as He went. But we can humbly choose to take the initiative and do the work He sets before us—but no breaking bad (boot-legging, drug dealing, or any other illegal activity). I'm pretty sure that wouldn't bring Him glory.

⁙ ⌒⟩ ✿ ⟨⌒ ⁙

Eyes on the Prize

I confess, when I consider my mom's life and her mom's and grandma's lives, I feel wimpy. My life has been so easy by comparison: no divorce, no tragic illnesses, no abandonment, or violence. Now please, understand me; I'm grateful for the blessing of family stability I've enjoyed. Oh, I've experienced trials and tears, but not the hardship they faced.

Life's end is like the last sprint of a marathon. Have my choices trained me for the long race ahead? When I choose the easy way, my resolve gets flabby. Task avoidance and pain aversion diminish determination. My husband, a former Marine, reminds me, "No pain? No gain! No guts? No glory!" We don't need easier lives; we need perseverance.

"Grow not weary in well doing for in due season you will reap if you faint not" (Galatians 6:9). This verse sustained me through the years I raised toddlers. Over and over, the Bible reminds us we need perseverance. Perseverance is a godly character trait. To never give up, never give in, to keep on keeping on, that's perseverance. As good as perseverance is, I want more. I want resilience. Resilience is perseverance with a twinkle in your eye and a skip in your step. It's moving forward in the joy of the Lord, no matter how tough the trail or heavy the load.

Resilience Wins

The first centenarian birthday party I ever attended was Rose Anna's. Friends from St. Elizabeth's and many extended family members made up the modest celebration. We were around forty or fifty in all, but many had come across the country to show their love to the woman they called mama, mémère, or tante (aunt). Five generations gathered that day. Many of us knew this would be the last time we saw her. Rose Anna enjoyed every minute of that party. She even took a comb, covered it with wax paper, and played *Take Me out to the Ball Game* on it. Her skill at making music with a poor man's harmonica had dwindled, but her enthusiasm had not. When she failed to carry the tune on the comb, she began to sing. The band started playing back up to her vocals. Her blind eyes twinkled. Her foot tapped the beat. The rest of us swayed in delight, glad to hear her sing it for the last time.

Over twenty years have come and gone since that celebration, but Rose Anna's treadle machine graces my living room, daily reminding me of her. I am the third owner. My grandma Irène gave it to me about twenty-five years ago. The oak case appears sturdy yet lovely, adorned with fancy carving, standing firm on a cast-iron frame. The antique, black sewing machine bears Singer's gilded trademark, and it still works when you pump the peddle. Rose Anna even put a "new" leather strap in one of its six tiny drawers. She planned to replace the old one when it wore out. Like my treadle machine, resilience doesn't quit; it retains its luster. Rose Anna owned that outstanding quality.

Growing the grand trait of resilience requires us to make hard choices. It's not easy to balance sorrow and joy, to be flexible and to be industrious. But without developing these habits of choice, we won't even persevere, let alone be resilient.

Choice Meditations

1. Consider Jeremiah 12:5. Explain what the author is asking in your own words.

2. What do you learn about strength and wisdom in Proverbs 24:5,6, and 10?

3. Read Isaiah 40:28–31. What encouragement do you find here?

4. What principle does Proverbs 14:23 teach?

5. Consider Romans 5:3. What does God intend for tribulation to produce in us?

Choice Considerations

1. How do you react to trials?

2. When you are going through trials, is your focus on your pain or the needs of others around you?

3. How could caring for those around us be a good diversion from our pain?

4. What has been the most difficult trial you faced? If you have come through, what did you gain through the process? If you're still in the struggle, what are you

learning?

Choice Actions

1. When I lived in Wisconsin, I wouldn't wear a coat until January. January and February are so frigid that if I didn't harden myself through December, I wouldn't be able to hack the worst of winter. Fasting is one way we can forsake comfort and prepare ourselves in and through difficult times. Do you desire to know the Lord more than food? Fast and pray; lay aside your convenience to get acquainted with the One who gives you strength.

2. Next time you have the opportunity to relieve someone of an unpleasant task, do it for them joyfully.

3. Resilience takes self-discipline. Start exercising or increase your current workout. If you don't exercise, consider parking at the farthest end of the lot and increase your number of daily steps. If you work out already, add another day to do thirty minutes of just cardio. My cardiac rehab nurse told me we should do thirty minutes of cardio exercise seven days a week! (Truth be told, I usually only get five in.)

7

Amiable Alba

Living Wealthy

(Sadie's oldest daughter)
"A man who has friends must himself be friendly, But there is a friend who sticks closer than a brother."
Proverbs 18:24

"**B**rian's finally starting to read on his own!" my mom informed me over a long-distance phone call.

"That's great. What happened?"

"We decided to visit Dad's Aunt Alba and her husband, Chet. She was a librarian, and when I told her about Brian's trouble with reading, she gave him some of Chet's Louis L'Amour novels. It turns out your brother enjoys them."

Enjoying books was a huge breakthrough for my eleven-year-old brother, who had difficulty learning to read. My mom spent hours teaching him in the evening because he just wasn't getting it in school. It also marked a turning point for my whole family. It was the first time they had ever gone to visit Aunt Alba. Oh, my dad had seen her a few times growing up, but his mom, Erma, and his aunt Lola had some disagreements along the way with Alba. As a result, the younger two sisters disassociated with Alba. At some point, my dad, who valued family ties and had become curious about his genealogy, decided it was time to get to know the oldest surviving Burton girl. That first visit began a series of visits over the years. My mother was eternally grateful for Alba's contribution to Brian's reading progress.

My son-in-law, an investment banker, will tell you the key to accumulating wealth lies in wise investments. This principle transcends finances. It applies to all forms of wealth. Alba knew how to invest. She invested in people. And she invested *generously*.

Alba's first child came into the world with spina bifida. Born in the 1940s, long before intrauterine treatment was possible, her little boy lived only nine months. They never had another biological child. So, they opted to adopt a son. I can't think of anything more generous than adopting a child—giving your home, love, and family name to a child with nothing. Adoption illustrates the love of God. The Bible tells us God adopts those of us who receive His forgiveness through Christ. He brought us into His family and called us His children, just like Alba and Chet claimed Henry as their child.

Henry ended up two thousand miles away from his parents. They lived in Idaho, and he landed in Michigan. School, job, and eventually family kept Alba's only son two thousand miles from her for the rest of her life. His annual visits to see his folks ended when his firstborn son, who had cerebral palsy, grew too big to be carried up Alba's stairs. She could no longer enjoy having her son and grandchildren come to her house. Despite their deep mutual love, their visits became rare as the years wore on. This disappointment didn't jade Alba's generosity. She continued to hold things with open hands.

Choose to be Generous

"Only two things will last forever: The Word of God and people's souls. Invest in the things that last." My husband has challenged every congregation he's pastored with this admonition. Good investing is a risky business. How many companies go bankrupt? Think about wealthy investors who lost everything in the Great Depression. Anytime you give something away, there's no guarantee you'll get it back, let alone with interest. You can play it safe with money and keep what you have, but our hearts don't work that way. The only sure thing to invest in is God's Word. As for people—they often fail us. People, all people, even you and me, disappoint others. We are sinners, yet God risked His Son knowing not all would choose salvation. Even those He saves fail to choose His will at times. I guarantee that if you invest in people, you will get hurt. Generosity invests in others—without expectation of return.

Some people will break your heart; others will defraud you. You may never receive a scrap of gratitude. So, don't serve anyone if you're looking for appreciation. Especially God, because the minute you give your heart to Him, He'll compel you to love others. "Where your treasure is, there your heart will be also," Jesus reminded His disciples (Matthew 6:21).

Treasure follows our hearts. When we choose to give our hearts, our time and possessions will follow. When we give generously to others, our investment secures *their* prosperity—not ours. We may never gain anyone's appreciation. That's okay because our reward comes from our Father's "Well done!" Yes, investing in people positions us for hurt and loss. But high-risk investments yield the highest rewards. Generous people invest for the benefit of others. And some even gain interest in their investments—interest *in* them, *not* from them.

Alba's Wonderful Curiosity

Alba enjoyed meeting characters and visiting places through well-written books. This farm girl from southern Idaho discovered the wonder of the world through words. Her love of books led her to become a librarian in a small town just a few hours from where she grew up, but her life was far from provincial. She traveled extensively and enjoyed making new acquaintances until the day she died at the age of one hundred.

On one of my parents' visits with Alba, my mom witnessed a habit Alba had developed. Alba noticed a neighborhood boy coming down her street and went outside to greet him.

"Hello, young man!"

"Hello, Mrs. Arndt," came his polite reply.

"I believe you have a birthday coming up soon, don't you?" she inquired.

"Yes, ma'am, next week."

Alba reached into her wallet and handed the lad a ten-dollar bill (another demonstration of her big-hearted nature), "Happy Birthday! Now don't forget to come by on your birthday. I'll have cookies and milk ready for you, and we can celebrate it together."

"I'll be here right after school!" he assured her.

"Just be sure you tell your mom you're coming here on your way home, okay?"

"Yes, Mrs. Arndt. I'll tell her."

Alba took a genuine interest in the details of peoples' lives. She knew all her neighbors' birthdays and made a point to show her regard.

Long before I met Alba, she would ask my folks about me and my family. Her interest in us was genuine, and she thought of ways she could invest in us. On occasion, she sent them home with goodies for my family. Alba saw an out-of-print children's book illustrated by my mom's favorite artist and gave it to my mother to pass on to my kids. Giving the book not only encouraged my kids to read but helped them get to know their grandma. The book, *The Little Indian and the Angel,* illustrated by De Grazia, provided my mom with a teaching moment as she explained why she appreciated this artist. "De Grazia burned his paintings before he died because his children could not afford to pay the inheritance tax. His extreme action led to inheritance tax reform," my mom explained to my children.

During one of my parents' visits, Alba passed a few gifts to each of my children and me. She selected a few items from her personal belongings that she thought we might enjoy. She wanted us to know she took an interest in us. One, in particular, surprised me. I lifted the ornate brass latch on the small case; six delicate, silver-plated teaspoons sat inside the velvet-lined box. I gasped. Such a treasure from a virtual stranger? She purchased the spoon set as a souvenir in England when I was just a baby.

I felt honored to be the recipient of such a prized possession. Keep in mind Alba had a daughter-in-law and two granddaughters whom she loved deeply, yet, she chose to give the heirloom silver pieces to me. She knew from getting to know me through my mom that I would enjoy these lovely little teaspoons and use them to have tea parties with my girls. Alba paid attention to the details of people because she took an interest in them.

Choose to be Interested in Others

When it comes to investing financially, it helps to understand the investment. The same principle applies to relationships. The more attention you give to people, the better you know them. The better you understand people, the more meaningful your investment in their lives. As a young mom, I felt compelled to pray that I would be a student of my children and husband. I was genuinely interested in their unique personalities, hopes and dreams, preferences, and opinions. I can't say I understand any of them perfectly. I can say I know them better because I made an effort to know them well.

Alba's curiosity made her a good student of people. She took the time to get to know folks. That grand choice involves many small choices. If I choose to be interested in others, it requires me to consider their well-being, not just my own. Hmm, it seems I've read that before in my Bible; sounds like Philippians chapter two. It means I must choose to listen to them in conversation and process what they're telling me. I can't pretend to hear them while listening to my thoughts, waiting to interject. Please, tell me I'm not the only one who does this. We must work toward active listening. For some individuals, this labor can feel worse than childbirth. Let's face it; there are people we don't find interesting and a few we find repulsive. But Jesus took an interest in all of humanity. He took the time to understand each person He encountered. To this day, He lives ever to make intercession for us, understanding what our actual needs are. Christ sacrificed His life for ours. Being genuinely interested in others will, at times, require sacrifice.

Meeting the Richest Woman in Haley

Alba and my Grandma Erma had already arrived at Lola's for Lola's ninetieth birthday celebration. I enjoyed many visits with Aunt Lola, but this was my first with Aunt Alba. She looked just like her mom. The same bright blue eyes I remember seeing on my great-grandmother's face twinkled at me. Identical fluffy snow-white hair covered Alba's head. She even had the same bone structure and smile as Sadie. Her voice carried the familiar tone of kindness I heard in Great-Grandma's. Her impeccable manner extended appropriate pleasantries—no please or thank you forgotten. Her eyes, though almost blind, looked directly at the person speaking. Her face was rapt with attention, straining to hear because her ninety-four-year-old ears were hard of hearing. A few years later, Alba consistently revealed these pleasant qualities on her hundredth birthday. She greeted every guest with grace and sincerity.

My favorite Christmas movie is *It's a Wonderful Life.* The last scene always brings me to tears when Gorge Baily's younger brother, Henry, arrives in his Air Force uniform after flying to George's rescue in a blizzard and gives a toast, "To my big brother, George, the richest man in town!" George is about to be thrown in jail for embezzlement because his forgetful uncle had lost the deposit for his savings and loan company. George was a man in dire financial straits. What did Henry mean when he called his brother the wealthiest man in town? The final scene is George opening a note from his guardian angel, Clarence, who makes it crystal clear. "Dear George, Remember, no man is a failure who has friends. Thanks for the wings! Love Clarence." George's friends opened their wallets, purses, and bank accounts to bail him out. True friends are better than money in the bank. And Alba was loaded.

A middle-aged woman, Alba's former student over thirty years before, traveled over eight hundred miles from Arizona to Idaho to tell Alba happy birthday. Upon her arrival, she heaped a pile of gold in Alba's lap, presenting her with a bouquet of one hundred bright yellow roses. This woman thanked my great aunt for being such a great teacher. How's that for a new gold standard?

Later that afternoon, we gathered at Alba's home for her annual birthday party. She threw herself one every year. To her, every life was worth celebrating, including her own. Every person in town came by, people of all ages. I asked one middle school boy how he knew my aunt. "I mow her grass." He told me. I asked a young woman how she knew my Aunt. "I come by to read her mail to her." Macular degeneration left Alba almost blind. Many who lose their eyesight in old age feel defeated and deprived. Not Alba. She never lacked a friend to serve as her eyes.

What surprised me most was that most of Alba's guests were younger. There wasn't much white hair in the crowd that day. Think about it. By the time a person reaches one hundred, they have few peers left. Alba never quit making friends. She never felt she had too many people in her life. She didn't mind if her friends were half her age or just a tiny fraction of it. Alba treasured people.

Choose True Wealth

The love we give to others, the influence for good we have in another's life, and the deep, meaningful friendships we make by investing and taking an interest in people—this is the wealth I want to accumulate. It means I must be aware of the people around me and learn to anticipate their needs. It means I need to make an effort to remember names. It amazes me how a stranger serving me responds with delight when I read their name tag and address them by name. We all long for appreciation as an individual who matters. When we choose to learn someone's name, it speaks volumes to them. I discovered this when Bill and I came to Grace Baptist Church.

Before moving to Kansas, I got a copy of the church's picture directory and began studying it. I looked at the faces of people I'd never met and prayed for each one by name. The Lord blessed that effort. Over and over again, different members of Grace shared their surprise at how quickly Bill and I remembered their names. They were impressed with how many other people we remembered and knew. All I can say is that I made a small effort, but God multiplied the results. He gets the glory!

God reveals His heart for people by knowing the number of hairs on our heads and knitting each one of us in our mother's womb. By declaring us His image-bearers, He valued people above all other created beings. The Lord deems us worthy of a priceless redemption bought by the blood of Christ. He paid top dollar for broken merchandise. Now, if that doesn't make us feel loved, nothing will. And if that doesn't motivate us to see the value of others, nothing else can. Since God finds people that worthwhile, shouldn't we? Simple practices like remembering birthdays, favorite colors, and food preferences honor people. Understanding their goals, sorrows, and fears reveals how much we value them.

Alba Saved the Best for Last

Just nine months after Alba's hundredth birthday, I found myself back in Haley for her funeral. The freezing, gray day made the sunshine and warmth of her June party seem like a dream. I had only one reason to come back—to be with Aunt Lola. I would be her only blood relative present, the only one who could hold her and share her sense of loss. Lola, the last Burton girl, I needed to be with her because *she* needed me there.

Together we celebrated Alba's life for the last time. Lola and I shared our family memories and said our goodbyes to this amiable woman she called sister and I called great aunt. Sitting in the

Catholic church where Alba had worshipped most of her life, we heard joyful melodies. It felt so unlike the gloomy Catholic funerals I had attended before. Musicians played on acoustic stringed instruments and sang with skilled voices—good hymns of hope. Alba made it a priority all her life to celebrate life. This memorial service was her last celebration and maybe her best. Her spirit no doubt celebrated with us. Friends and neighbors filled every pew. She would have offered us tissues if she could have. Every mourner wept.

The graveside service on that frigid February day proved just as crowded. Yet only four family members came: Lola, Henry (Alba's only child), my mom (an in-law), and me. My acquaintance with Alba was brief. Yet, her life touched mine and affected me profoundly. As I sat grieving for Alba, the treasure that made her the wealthiest woman in Haley, Idaho, glittered before my eyes—her multitude of friends. They wept too, their loss no doubt greater than mine. They lost a gem, an irreplaceable, precious stone of their community. Alba's attributes are rare in our present time of disconnect. Social media via the internet deludes us into feeling more connected—but we are not. We seldom enjoy real presence with real people like Alba did.

Now she is gone, and we are poorer for it; but she left us singing and looking up to her Father, God. She saved the best, most important celebration for last; she celebrated not just life but *eternal* life at her funeral. And I do hope to see her again someday. Her final farewell spoke "I hope to see you later," to each of us present.

Choose to Celebrate Life

Let's choose to make much of small things, maybe a grandchild's schoolwork or a neighbor's freshly planted garden. Celebrate with ice cream or iced tea. Let's celebrate births, especially our own. Our lives matter. Throw parties, play games. Give away lots of smiles and presents. In all the celebrating we choose to do, let's be mindful of the life that should be celebrated most—life in Christ—*eternal* life. Let's share it and declare it! We can never make too much of Him because He has made much of us. Growing grand entails growing our appreciation of life and our ability to celebrate it.

Wisdom plans. It's wise to plan what we want to communicate at our last celebration. I'm convinced Alba planned her funeral. I've thought a lot about my funeral over the years. Now I just need to write it out and put the means in place to make it happen. What a party I want to throw for my family and friends. I want them to know they are loved and loved forever by the God Who made them—the One who will never leave or forsake them.

On that last visit to Haley, Alba's son, my cousin, Henry, let me pick a treasure from Alba's china hutch. I chose a child-sized tea set: pot, sugar bowl, and creamer. Ornate and fragile with brightly painted pink and yellow flowers, this delicate porcelain set reminds me of people and the importance of friendships. Our relationships can be beautiful, but they can also be fragile, like fine china and the beautiful silver teaspoons Alba gave me. Relationships need special care and, like the pieces of the tea set and the spoons, the more, the merrier. When gathered together, they make an elaborate party.

So, I will work at choosing to invest in people and taking a genuine interest in others. I will also choose to gather true riches. Friends. And as is my habit, I will continue to choose to celebrate life because nothing is grander than God's breath animating a human soul.

Choice Meditations

1. Ponder Proverbs 18:24. How do you show yourself friendly? How have others been friendly to you?

2. Job 16:20 and 19:13–21 illustrate the reality that even close friends sometimes fail us. I think it's worth noting that Job's story was recorded after the fact, and the scribe still records these men as friends. Even though they said hurtful things, Job was glad they cared enough to come. He never tells them to leave him alone or sets out to even the score. He waited for the Lord. Look at what happened in Job 42:7–9. Have you had a friendship end badly? How are you working toward reconciliation? How do you pray for them?

3. Read 1 Samuel 18:1–9. What do you discover about the beginning of this beautiful friendship? Read 2 Samuel 9:1–11. What do you learn about the riches of this friendship? How does this illustrate Proverbs 27:10? What did you learn about faithfulness as you consider these verses?

Choice Considerations

1. When was the last time you made a new friend? How long has your longest friendship lasted?

2. Do you have friends who are not your age? In a different place in life? Who are not in the same profession or income class as you are?

3. Do you have friends with different political views? Religious affiliations? Values?

4. How do you connect with people who are different than you?

5. How much time do you carve out to spend with friends and new acquaintances?

Choice Actions

1. Be intentional and plan to go to coffee or lunch twice each month, once with a good friend and once with a new acquaintance. You may do more, and that's great, but if you can't remember the last time you went out with a friend—it's been too long.

2. Keep a notebook (or at least a mental list) with personal information on your friends, like their birthdays, favorite colors, or authors.

3. Plan a surprise party for a friend who enjoys surprises (remember, not everyone does).

4. If you have an estranged friend, put her on your prayer list and begin asking God to reconcile the two of you.

5. Make much of little. Celebrate a small accomplishment in

a friend's life in a big way. Life is worth celebrating!

Remember this rhyme, "Make new friends, but keep the old. One is silver, the other gold."

8

Legendary Lola

Living Larger than Life

(Sadie's middle daughter)
"Most blessed of women be Jael, the wife of Heber the Kenite, of tent-dwelling women most blessed."
Judges 5:24

"She always brought home the most ribbons from the fair."

"She worked as hard as any man!"

"She always caught the biggest fish!"

"She could drop an elk bull with one rifle shot from horseback."

Who was she, this legendary woman? Lola Michaeline Burton Salveson, my great-aunt. Lola loomed larger than life when she came up in a family conversation. She was my father's favorite aunt and her husband, Orville, a.k.a. Bud, my dad's favorite uncle. Together Lola and Bud ran a cattle ranch south of Pocatello just outside the smaller than small town of Downey, Idaho. Much like the legendary Idaho potato picture in postcards—the giant potato that fills a semi-truck bed—Lola's reputation outsized her demure stature by several feet and pounds.

She stood five feet tall on the outside but dwarfed Goliath on the inside. Her petite frame, complimented by fair features and curly, burnt umber locks, made her quite a good-looking woman in her youth. Her dark eyes gleamed with steely resolve. Now, I'm not saying that Lola was stubborn, but I will say, her tenacity made a mule look compliant. Her feet were small but wide. Poor Lola. Finding sandals that fit was impossible for her. She liked painting her toenails red. Determined to show them off, she hired a doctor to amputate her little toes. "You can't see pinky toes in sandals anyway. Now I can find sandals that fit," Lola boasted.

At one point in writing this book, I googled my grandmother, Erma Burton Donaldson. Nothing about her came up. Instead, I found Lola Burton Salveson's obituary listing Erma as a sister who preceded her in death. I laughed. Then I got curious, so I googled Alba Burton Arndt, their older sister. I found several articles about her, followed by Lola's obituary. Just for fun, I googled Lola. Her obituary stood alone, with no articles about Erma and none about Alba either. I chuckled. It reminded me of that 4-H trophy my grandmother resented; even in death, Lola managed to stay on top. Erma and Alba remained mere dittos. Legendary souls tend to overshadow those around them, not intentionally. It's just what happens when they're living larger than life.

The third girl, not the boy her father longed for, Lola was named after him anyway, hence her middle name of Michaeline. She entered the world on Friday, the thirteenth of October, 1911. I wonder, was her father superstitious? Did Michael Burton think to have a third girl was a bit of bad luck? Either way, Lola was bound and determined to live up to his name and make him a proud papa. She loved farming with her father, especially caring for the animals. Lola had a wonderful way with creatures. Like Doctor Doolittle, Lola talked with the animals.

The first trip to Lola and Bud's that I can remember, I was all of three years old. "Uncle Bud and Aunt Lola have horses!" my dad informed me.

"Real horses? Can I see one?!"

"Yes, you will. Maybe you'll even get to ride one. The first time I rode a horse was at Aunt Lola's," Daddy announced.

At three, I was all cowgirl. I watched every episode of Annie Oakley on television. My little heart pitter-pattered as I imagined sitting on a live horse. I can still see Lola holding my hand as we headed out to the barnyard on that sunny summer morning the day after we arrived. The bright open sky lifted high overhead as we strolled across the lawn. The grass gave way to dirt as rough wooden fences set a corral boundary. Behind the barn, acres of wheat fields waved to distant mountains. Then he appeared with his head held high. Large eyes, bright as polished ebony, looked toward us. He clip-clopped straight to the fence, neighing his pleasure to see Lola.

"Teri, meet Tony. Tony, Teri." Lola handed me a carrot. The horse's eyes followed it like magnets. "Now you need to keep your hand flat, so he just takes the carrot, not your fingers. The hair on his lips will tickle a bit, but he won't hurt you." I balanced the carrot on my open hand and carefully lifted it to the horse's mouth. Tony stretched out his head as he lowered his white muzzle and flexed his nostrils to sniff the treat. His soft, velvet lips wisped across my palm. I felt the horse's warm breath; it smelt of hay. Then he crunched the carrot in his mouth. I had never been so close to such a large creature. My whole fist could fit into one of his nostrils and those teeth!

Tony stood sixteen hands, rather tall for a Morgan. The bay-colored horse sported a dandy white streak down the center of his face; it wrapped around his nose and mouth. He was a handsome old gentleman, about fifteen years old at that time. Lola trusted this horse to be careful with a first-time rider.

"Do you want to sit on him?" she asked.

"Oh yes!" I shrieked with pleasure, as only a child can.

Lola lifted me up with her strong arms and set me on Tony's bareback. Heated by the sun, his silky brown coat felt almost hot on my legs. I smelled his musky scent. Lola handed me the rope attached to Tony's bridle and took hold of his harness.

"Squeeze him tight with your legs. Dig your heels into his sides. You don't want to fall off." She warned. My feet didn't even reach the widest part of his belly, but I tried to do what Lola told me to. Then she clicked her tongue and led him around the yard. I felt the rhythm of his muscles tensing and relaxing, moving like the waves of the sea beneath me. I've never forgotten the thrill of my first horse ride, Tony's majestic form, and Lola's tender care for both of us.

This ranch was Lola's domain. Her home, her barnyard, her kingdom. She ruled it well. Lola dominated every task she undertook. Whether it was sewing, cooking, or training her dogs and horses, she mastered everything she put her hand to.

Choose to Take Dominion

Annie Oakley took dominion over her impoverished childhood by taking up a gun for survival. She needed to help put food on her widowed mother's table. She became quite a legendary sharpshooter. Her place in Wild Bill Hickock's Wild West Show gave her claim to fame as America's first female star. The television show I enjoyed as a child portrayed her as a law keeper in the wild west. I could find no evidence that she was a deputy, but that's the life of a legend. A story grows from a seed of truth. Then it outgrows the natural life-span of its main character.

Speaking of seed, Johnny Appleseed (John Chapman) covered the whole west with apple trees, or so the legend goes. He did introduce apple trees to large parts of Pennsylvania, Ohio, Indiana, and Illinois. Mr. Appleseed took dominion by planting orchards. He proved to be a kind-hearted, generous husbandman.

Colorful folk songs and tales celebrate his contribution to the westward migration of our country. Walt Disney, a legend in his own right, even made an animated movie about Johnny Appleseed.

To the Israelites, Jael became a legend when she killed their enemy with kindness. After feeding Sisera and lulling him to sleep, she took her hammer and tent pegs. The tools she had long used to dominate the hard, dry ground became weapons in her hands as she pierced the skull of Israel's persecutor. Her story appears in the book of Judges, chapters four and five. This gruesome tale reminds me again of Lola cutting off her pinky toes. In her domain, she would show off those pretty red toes no matter what it took!

From creation, God gave us dominion. He made us in His image, and part of bearing that image requires us to rule over our domain. Yes, Sisters, you and I were created to master. For those of us who are married, we partner as one with our husbands. Our place of submission is not a lesser position. We must secure the order of our homes. In so doing, we extend our husband's ability to have dominion outside the home. I don't believe a woman should only work at home. I do know if a woman's home is not well-ordered, she has no business exporting her skills to other domains. We need to get our priorities in line with our purpose. Once those are in order, it's all about domination!

My husband and I possess strong wills. While he was working on his doctorate, a professor who was certifying Bill to give the Taylor Johnson Temperament test had Bill test both of us for evaluation. The professor, stunned by the results, asked, "How do you two stay married?"

"Well," my sweet William responded, "we each know our domains. It works well as long as we stay in our realm of responsibility. We tend to get into trouble when we tread on each other's turf."

Within the first twelve months of matrimony, I remember an argument that went like this,

"I'm the head of this house!" my groom insisted.

"But," I retorted, "I'm the keeper of this home!"

I have no clue what the issue was. We resolved it long ago by understanding we were *both* right. God commissioned him to be the leader of our family. But God also appointed me with the crucial task of ordering our home. Home is the realm of wifely dominion.

Lunch at Lola's

"Let's get some dinner," said Lola as she and I traipsed out the door.

"Dinner?" I wondered. We had just finished breakfast.

Sunshine and crisp fall air greeted us as we stepped into the front yard of my great-aunt Lola's small ranch house. Chickens clucked and pecked. A blue Australian healer named Lady wagged her tail as she jogged over to say good morning to her mistress. We walked a few paces to the center of the lawn and stood quietly. Lady bid us adieu and trotted off to do whatever a cattle dog does when it isn't herding cattle. A whirl of white fluff, and scattering hens, clucking their uproar, took me by surprise. Lola wrung the neck of our dinner; I didn't even see her snatch the bird up. I stood amazed.

Witnessing her skill in wringing that bird's neck confirmed my opinion that Lola was a living legend. I had tried to catch her chickens. This game got me into trouble. "Don't get those chickens all worked up. It makes 'em tough and works the fat off 'em." Lola scolded.

I had never been able to grab one. I did succeed in making the rooster mad; then he'd chase me. Lola's long-developed technique grabbed our dinner in seconds, and she never chased a chicken. As for the rooster, he knew well enough to leave her alone.

Lola started off to the shed. I, being only eight, had already been distracted by the waiting adventures of the ranch. Curiosity about other things spared me the sight of plucking, skinning, and dressing the bird—skills a kid from suburbia had no use for. Well aware of my ignorance, Lola had no desire to ruin my appetite. For that mercy, I'm forever grateful. When she called me in for lunch, the aroma of fried chicken greeted me as I walked in the door. Nothing procured in a grocery store can come close to the taste of free-range, yard feed, fresh, fried chicken. And no one, not even Colonel Sanders, could fry chicken, quail, or pheasant, for that matter, like Lola. It tasted savory, the texture crisp, tender, and juicy, all in one bite. Lola's cooking skills had won her blue ribbons in fairs since she was a teenager. Young men and boys coveted a position as Bud's hire hands so that they could eat at Lola's table. But culinary skill was not the only factor in Lola's fame.

When I was young, maybe seven or eight, a package arrived in the mail addressed to me. It wasn't my birthday or Christmas. "What kind of present is it?" I wondered. The return address identified the sender, Lola Salveson. I tore the brown paper from the box and ripped through the tape. I carefully unwrapped the layers of white tissue paper. Lola sent me an outfit for my Barbie doll. She crocheted the fitted, knee-length dress from winter-white yarn and belted it at the waist by quarter-inch red velvet ribbon tied in a bow. Lola sewed a red velvet cape lined in black and white herringbone wool as the outer layer of the ensemble. The conservative style left my immature taste in fashion unimpressed. After all, it wasn't even an evening gown, no hot pink or neon orange, no sparkle, ruffles, or lace. After reading Lola's letter that accompanied the gift, my mom knew my attitude needed to be adjusted. I lacked appropriate appreciation for this gift.

"Lola made this doll outfit and entered it in the county fair. It won first place, you know. You should feel proud to have it. The judges felt this was the best-made dress out of all the entries. Lola could have sent it to your cousin Kathy, but she wanted you to have it. You should be thankful. Someday you'll appreciate how special it is," my mother admonished sternly. Mom was right. It became one of my favorite outfits to put on Barbie. I still have this treasure. My three daughters used it too. Unfortunately, moths nibbled at the wool, and now it has a couple of tiny holes. But I don't doubt at least one more generation will enjoy Lola's skilled handiwork.

One of my favorite Aunt Lola stories I didn't hear until after her death. A woman at Lola's memorial service shared how Lola had been her 4-H sewing teacher. "If you did it wrong, she'd make you rip out every bad stitch, then teach you how to get it right. Lola was a perfectionist. Lola's 4-H kids always took home ribbons from the fair." Then she told the story of her wedding dress.

"I had picked out a beautiful French pattern. It didn't take me long to see I was in over my head. I took it to Lola in tears because I only had a few days to finish it. "Please, Lola, will you help me?" She assured me she would. The next day she showed up with the dress. My wedding dress. It was not only finished; it was *perfect*. It looked exactly like the picture and fit me like a glove. I thought Lola would just help me with the hard parts, but no, she sewed the whole dress. And it only took her one night to do it."

As if cooking, sewing, and crocheting weren't enough, Lola knew how to fish too. Now, I confess she never took me fishing. I rely, at this point, on legend alone. Yet, after listening to her funeral, a list of Lola's skills would be incomplete without singing her praise as a fisherwoman. She knew the importance of balancing work and rest. Fishing refreshed her soul. The quiet creeks around her home provided a stillness, a break from the breakneck pace of ranching. Fishing developed patience in her. She knew how to out-wait anyone. Lola worked just as hard at her play as at her work. That's how she always caught the biggest fish and always caught fish when no one else got a bite on their line.

Lola was a jack of all trades and master of most. If she chose to do something, she chose to do it well. Domination requires skill. Lola mastered many skills because she worked hard at them. She worked to compete and worked harder to win, but she worked hardest to serve those she loved.

Choose to Develop Skill

Lola's motivations remain a mystery to me. As far as I could tell, Lola did not have faith in Christ. As a believer, I know I'm called to let my light shine and to do everything for God's glory. That's why choosing to be skilled in my endeavors is vital to me. Sloppy work brings glory to no one, but the one who is "skilled will stand before kings," Solomon wrote. I wonder, did he have his father in mind as he penned this proverb?

David, the giant killer, a legend in his own time, developed skill with his sling. David stood before King Saul, proclaiming, "To protect my father's flock, I have killed both a lion and a bear. I will kill this Philistine also." And he did!

I have not mastered many skills like my great-aunt, Lola. I'm a Jill of all trades but a mistress of none. I possess plenty of raw talent but little drive, a classic underachiever. Lola, on the other hand, was the overachiever poster child. By nature, I'm a sloth; by nurture, I plan to be a busy bee and produce lots of sweet things. Overcoming twenty years of laziness to become skilled for the glory of God has not been easy. I love Orville Redenbacher's motto, "Pick one thing, and do it better than anyone." One thing! I think I can handle one thing, but which thing? I like doing so many different things. So, rather than trying to pick one and "do it better than anyone," I'll choose One audience and work for His praise instead of people's praise. I'll decide to do an excellent job at whatever I'm doing and work to hear my Father's voice say, "Well done!" That's a better prize than any ribbon. Ribbons fade, but God's glory lasts forever.

Working for God's glory means I must choose not to be lazy. No procrastination. I need to choose perseverance too. Starting is easy. But finishing? That's hard! I need to learn from my mistakes for God to be glorified in my work. Failure is inescapable; we either embrace it as a faithful friend who teaches us how to change, or we find it a discouraging foe who makes us want to quit. I choose to embrace Thomas Edison's view of failure. When asked by a reporter how he felt about his 10,000 failed attempts at making a light bulb, Edison said these were not failures, just 10,000 steps in the process of making a light bulb. Let's allow failure to be the friend that leads us to success.

Skill and talent work well together, but developing a skill does not require talent. We learn skills. Learning a skill requires a teachable attitude. I can master a skill if I choose to watch, listen, and receive correction. I never earned a college degree, but I've taken many classes and read many books. I go to writer's conferences and soak up all the constructive criticism I can get. I am learning to be a skilled writer. You're reading this book because I learned how to become an author. Quite frankly, it's been the hardest thing I've ever done—and I delivered two of my four children without medication. The labor of writing a book seems excruciating and never-ending, but I've chosen to write for the glory of God. Hence, I choose to persevere and develop the skills this task requires. Choosing to take dominion and learning to work with skill take another character trait: tenacity.

Tough as Nails and Twice as Sharp

"Lola worked as hard as any man twice her size." When did I first hear this? Who told me? My dad? My grandma? I don't know. I do know I heard it a lot growing up. Lola was a strong woman. I never witnessed feats of her legendary physical strength. I did see her inner strength, the tenacity that set her apart.

I managed to attend Lola's ninetieth birthday, quite the family affair. My dad, his brothers, my grandma, and my great-aunt Alba came. It had been over twenty years since I had last seen Lola. Now at ninety, her hair was shining white. Her skin resembled well-tanned leather, parched by years of exposure, but the steely gleam in her eyes remained untouched by the years. After everyone else had gone to bed, Lola and I stayed up past 1:00 a.m. renewing our relationship. We talked about all kinds of things. At some point, she asked, "Am I as old as my sisters? They are so old!" her voice fraught with doubt.

"Lola, you'll never be old," came from my mouth without hesitation. "You are grand, not old."

Relief replaced her concerned expression. I confirmed what she knew. She just needed to hear it; she was not old. Physical bodies break down over time, but the passing of time has little effect on the core of our eternality, our soul. This explains why many aged people say, "I don't feel any different inside. I'm the same person I've always been." A tenacious soul fights the outer decay by clinging to the reality that they are more than flesh. They rely on the strength and perpetual youth of their soul. "Therefore, we do not lose heart. Even though our outward man is perishing, yet the inward man is being renewed day by day" (2 Corinthians 4:16). A few days later, I witnessed another feat of Lola's will.

It was a blustery fall day in Idaho as I traipsed with Lola across the street to the tiny house my great-grandma, Sadie, once occupied. Lola now rented it out. Her tenant was out of town, and she agreed to keep an eye on the place. My hands grew clammy as I mustered up the courage to engage Lola in a sensitive matter. "I know it's none of my business, but there's something I've always wondered about."

"Spit it out, girl!" Lola replied.

"Why didn't you and Uncle Bud ever have children? You loved kids so much." There I asked! Had I hurt her or angered her? Would she be tearful or yell? I didn't know what to expect; I only knew I wanted to know. I loved her. She had already lived nine decades; this may well be my last chance to get the facts of her life straight. I wanted her life remembered accurately. I intended to carve her true legacy on our family tree. She had no children of her own to do it, and she had been far grander to me than her sister, Erma, my grandmother.

"Well, my uterus was about the size of a kidney bean. When my monthly cycle came around, there'd be just enough blood to fill a thimble." Her tone sounded matter of fact, her manner unflappable. "We just couldn't. So, I loved other folk's kids, and that was fine with me."

"I'm sorry."

"Why?"

"I asked my grandma once. She didn't know. I'm sure if you never told her, it must have been painful to see her having children when you couldn't," I stammered.

"I never told her because she never asked."

"Maybe I shouldn't have asked," I continued.

"No, I permitted you to ask a personal question. And I'm glad you did. You should know."

I don't doubt Lola struggled with a deep sense of hurt and loss over her bareness. She was, after all, a competitive woman who loved children. And to top it off, she lived her whole life in a small town whose population was 99.9% Mormon. Yes, you heard me. She was immersed in a culture that equates a woman's worth to her fertility.

Raised by a Catholic father and a Presbyterian mother, Lola's family was the only one in town that was not Mormon. She married a Mormon man who faithfully paid a tithe to his ward but nothing more. They were not Mormons in practice, and they had no children. Yet, Lola continued to be involved in her community. She lived committed to loving her neighbors. She refused to buckle under any judgment that came her way. Her strong will and sharp wit made her a force to be contended with. And in the end, her tenacity gained her the respect and affection of her neighbors.

Lola chose to celebrate her nine decades of life by doing something she hadn't done in quite a while. She made us, along with her closest friends, a turkey dinner with all the fixings. It must have been at least twenty years since Lola cooked for such a large crew. I can still see her carrying out that twenty-pound platter loaded with a golden, roasted bird. Her thin, tawny muscles flexed beneath the wrinkled skin of her arms while her steady grip set the tasty treasurer on the table. Lola hadn't lost her touch. The meal she made to honor us and celebrate her life tasted *delicious*.

I also remember my grandma Erma's protest. "Lola, it's your birthday, we should go out. You shouldn't have to cook."

"I don't have to cook! It's my birthday, and I *want* to cook." She declared. "Besides, what restaurant can make a tastier meal than me?"

The answer is none!

Lola is the biggest little gal I have ever met. She and my great-aunt Alba came for a rare visit to celebrate my grandma Erma's ninetieth birthday. At ninety-three, Lola stood as straight as an arrow with a wit twice as sharp. Gravity had stolen inches off both Alba and Erma's height. Both of Lola's sisters stooped with hunched backs, victimized by osteoporosis. Not Lola! She retained every inch of her sixty-inch stature. More tenacious than age and gravity, she kept her muscles strong.

"Stretch your back every morning," she told my mom and me. "I scooch to the bottom of my bed, then reach my arms up, grab the top of the mattress, and pull myself up every morning." She also walked all over town every day. She lived to be a hundred one and died with a mind sharp as a tack.

I could not attend her funeral, but the executor of her estate sent me an audio recording. The service included an open time of sharing. As a pastor's wife who's been to many funerals, I know this can be risky. You never know what people will say when someone's died and isn't there to hear. Over and over, I heard testimonies of Lola's love. "She was a second mother to me," turned out to be a common thread in the small town of Downey. Barren Lola ended up with more kids calling her mom than most women ever have. And she did it with a uterus the size of a kidney bean and a heart as big as a barn. Now that's living large, larger than life!

Choose to be Tenacious

Growing up in the sixties, I listened to a lot of folk music. My dad was fond of The New Christy Minstrels. One of his favorite songs was the Ballad of John Henry and the Steam Drill. The ballad tells the story of the competition between man and machine: "muscle and metal against the mountain." John Henry wins, but it kills him. The legendary John Henry, born with a hammer in his hand, stands out as America's marvel of tenacity. When it comes to hammering in the Bible, it's a woman who stands out, Jael. She and Lola knew how to flex their muscles, but both were content to be women. They both knew their way around a kitchen and how to feed hungry men. We don't know if Jael had children; none are mentioned. Therefore, I can safely say both Jael and Lola found identities apart from motherhood.

Lola didn't need to be a mother to see herself as a woman. In her role as a wife, she was Uncle Bud's equal. She didn't let roles or social obligations define her. By embracing her unique self, Lola established her identity. She embraced the woman in her skin. She had the tenacity to be true to herself, to stand on her own two feet.

Who are we apart from our relationships and abilities? These can prove to be shaky ground in building an identity. God created human relationships for time, but He made us, as individuals, for eternity. In time, we may or may not find a husband and have or not have children. In time, we may outlive our husbands and children. In time, accidents and illness may steal our talents, abilities, and mobility. If we find our identity in these things, and they disappear, then who are we? Being a mother doesn't make you a woman. We need to remember motherhood may be part of who we are but it's not what defines us. Our identity goes beyond the people we parent or even the men we marry. Living larger than life comes from viewing our own life as unique. God made each of us in his image. Each person shines as a facet of the gem God is.

Choosing to be tenacious means I choose to embrace the person God made me; I cling to my attributes, good and bad. I own both my successes and failures. I must stand before God alone to give account. When I stand before the Lord, He will not ask me about my husband's and children's choices. He will hold me accountable for the choices I make. I want to have the resolve to make good choices. Tenacious women learn to stand alone.

Thirty years ago, I could juggle a baby and a toddler while bringing in groceries. I could dig, prune, and haul debris out of my yard all day. I lifted boxes in and out of many a moving van. My young body glowed with perspiration, and well-toned muscle defined my physique. Physically, I was a strong woman and didn't have to work at it. Hard work kept me strong. Then my children grew, and my jobs changed. Life became less strenuous. The muscles I wasn't using, I was losing.

The aging process robs our bodies of physical strength. That's where I find myself both physically and mentally now that I've reached my sixties. Diminishing strength took me by surprise. Maintaining my physical strength requires twice as much effort as it used to. This extra workout takes more determination. My strength may be failing, but I can choose tenacity. I can cling to a workout routine that allows me to maintain some muscle tone. Lola did.

As for emotional strength, feelings of insecurity that could not have touched my heart twenty years ago now derail my progress in moving forward in this new phase of my life. Who knew having an empty nest would be so challenging? I have less work, but I also have less energy, strength, and courage. Time to start making hard choices. Choices like working out daily or at least doing a thirty-minute cardio walk four times a week. I must dominate my domain by keeping my house and yard in order. I'm not Lola. I will leave *my* legacy, a different legacy than Lola's. Will my story become a family legend? I will never know, and that's okay. After all, a legend is just a story, the tale of someone tenacious, taking dominion and developing skill. We all have a story. We all have choices to make.

Ruth, one of my favorite Bible characters, chose to be tenacious. When she and her mother-in-law, Naomi, found themselves widowed and destitute, Naomi decided to head back home to Bethlehem. She encouraged her daughters-in-law to go back to their homes too. Orpah went, but not Ruth. Beckoned by the Almighty, Ruth clung to Naomi with a tenacious spirit. The word "clung" in Ruth 1:14 is the same word used in Genesis 2, which speaks of a man cleaving to his wife. Like a bulldog sinks his teeth into a bone and won't let go, Ruth joined herself to God and committed to caring for Naomi. I want that same tenacity as I follow God.

Physical and mental tenacity may come naturally. But don't fret; if you don't have it, choose to stick with things and grow tenacious. The writer of the book of Hebrews reminds us, "we have need of endurance," the strength to keep on keeping on. Only power will keep us going when life wears us out and tears us down, but whose? When we exhaust our muscles and resolve, when our strength is gone, then what? Paul reminded the saints in Ephesus, "Be strong in the Lord and in the power of His might." My weakness requires me to cling to God tenaciously. After all, His "strength is perfected in my weakness." Apart from Him, I can do nothing, at least nothing of eternal value.

When December comes around, my Christmas tree stands adorned with Idaho snowflakes that never melt. These white lace beauties didn't fall from the sky. They fell in a flurry from the fast-moving crochet hook held in Lola's hands. Each one is unique, just like the ones God makes. Each one skillfully crafted, leaving me a legacy, a reminder. "Choose to take dominion!" cries the thread dominated by Lola's hand. "Choose to develop a skill." declare the beautiful white creations. "Choose to be tenacious!" proclaim the snowflakes that never melt. In a chorus, they herald, "Live grand like Lola. Live larger than life!"

Choice Meditations
1. Read Genesis 1:26–27. What task did God give men and women? What do you discover about the value of each gender?

2. Read Genesis 3:1–8. How did Eve fail to take dominion over the serpent? What did that cost her?

3. Consider 2 Corinthians 10:4–6 and 2 Timothy 3:1–7. How important is it to have dominion over our own thought life?

4. Hebrews 11 is often referred to as the Hall of Faith. Read this chapter. As you consider the saints listed here, describe how their faith displayed tenacity.

Choice Considerations

1. In what ways are you satisfied with your homemaking? What areas of housekeeping feel out of control to you?

2. Concerning your worth and purpose, would you say you more often feel equal, inferior, or superior to others? How does the truth that every human being is made to bear God's image affect your feelings of worth and purpose? How is this truth a liberating equalizer?

3. What skills have you developed over the years? What new skills are you developing? What skill would you like to establish before you die?

4. When something becomes difficult, do you meet the challenge and persevere, or do you give up? How did perseverance pay off? What disappointment came with quitting?

Choice Actions

1. Pick one area of your home that feels out of control, and make attainable, measurable goals to get it back in order.

Try planning backward. What do you want in the end? What must happen first, then next, and so on? Write it out. Include target dates for each step. The goal is your ruler; the steps serve as inch marks. Remember, *it's hard by the yard, but a cinch by the inch!*

2. If you haven't used an old skill for a while, plan time on your calendar to work on it. Read a book on the subject or take a class.

3. Choose one skill and work at it a few minutes every day. *Don't give up!*

4. Make sure you are developing the skill of understanding God through His Word. Be tenacious in spending time with Him daily. If this has not been your habit, pick one fifteen-minute slot in your day to read His word and pray. Maybe at breakfast? After all, Jesus is the Bread of Life. Enjoy Him as your first meal of the day!

5. One last idea—remember Lola's counsel, "Stretch your back out every morning before you get out of bed."

PART 3

The Guests

Stories of a neighbor, an acquaintance, and friends who became mentors.
I treasured their memories as valued guests in my heart.

9

Radiant Ruth

Living with an Open Door

Let brotherly love continue.
Do not neglect to show hospitality to strangers,
for thereby some have entertained angels unawares.
Hebrews 13:1–2

Coming home from work one day, I crossed paths with the resident manager of the apartments where I lived. He looked perturbed as he burst into the hall between our apartments.

"Stan, what's wrong?" I asked.

"It's old, Mrs. Grant. She's half deaf and can't hear her teakettle whistle. So, the fire alarm is going off. *Again!* Third time this week!"

As Stan stomped off, I sighed with relief. Yay! He wasn't mad at me.

I didn't know Mrs. Grant. She was just another of the many residents in our two-building apartment complex—just another annoyance to Stan. He once confided in me he had only taken the job for free rent. He found many of us annoying. I disregarded his opinions of people—including Mrs. Grant.

Several months later, I bumped into Stan again.

"Hey Teri, I know you're tired of your studio in the basement. There's a one-bedroom in the other building that's going to be available on the first. You want it?"

"Sure!" I jumped at the offer of more space and sunlight. But the best thing about that move was meeting my new neighbor, Ruth Grant.

I trudged to my new apartment building late one afternoon. After working all day on my feet, the twenty-minute walk home in the Tacoma drizzles left me limp. I wanted to wilt into my pajamas and easy chair for the night, but God planned something better. As I pulled the heavy oak entry door open, a whistling teakettle caught my ear. It sounded from the apartment just to the right of the lobby door.

"Hmmm, must be the home of the infamous Mrs. Grant," I thought.

Curious, I stopped to listen. Would the owner of the kettle tend to it? Seconds crept by as I listened and waited. The full steam whistle died down to a quiet sputter. Soon the water would fizzle away, and smoke would replace the steam. I pounded on the door. A pale brown eye stared at me through the peephole briefly before the door creaked open.

A woman many decades my senior cautiously peered up at me. I'm around five foot three; time and gravity had taken a toll on Mrs. Grant's stature. Her countenance, however, radiated warmth. Her hair resembled fluffy white clouds—a stark contrast to the weather outside. Soft curls framed her smile-lined face. The lines bore witness to the many smiles she wore through the years. Her eyes, dimmed with age, reminded me of the color of hot cocoa. I imagined those eyes were once like a couple of dark chocolate kisses. Time faded the hue of her eyes but not the twinkle; her wire-rimmed bifocals magnified the size and shine of her peepers. Her winsome features captivated me.

"May I help you?" she asked.

"Your kettle is whistling," I replied in a raised voice so she could hear.

She glanced back to her stove, "Oh, so it is. Thank you for telling me." Her gaze returned to me. "Would you care to join me for a cup of tea?"

Who was this little old lady who had invited a stranger into her home? We lived in downtown Tacoma, with a crime rate resembling Gotham City's when Batman was on vacation. Curiosity overtook my fatigue. Ruth's radiant disposition drew me into her open door as I accepted her kind hospitality.

Tidy surroundings greeted me, a clue to her work ethic. I noticed a piano in the corner. Did she play? Pictures of people she cared about covered her mantel. Did they care for her too?

Choose to Be Brave

Inviting a stranger into one's home is a risky business. Ruth Grant had good reason not to ask me in at her age. But she took the risk, knowing the potential for reward. Ruth's bold example reminds me of the New Testament call to hospitality. Hospitality relates to the new faces we see at church, the strangers who knock at our doors, and the neighbors we haven't met yet. *Philonexia*, the Greek word for *hospitality* used in Hebrews 13:2, is not God's friends-and-family-plan. "It is useful to limit the meaning of 'hospitality' to benevolence done to those outside one's normal circle of friends, as is implied in the literal meaning of the Greek word ('love of strangers')."[1] We American Christians tend to forget the true meaning of hospitality.

We throw this term around when it comes to hosting our care group, Bible study, or inviting our pastor over. Those are important ways to "Let brotherly love continue," but hosting a party for people we know falls short of biblical hospitality. It's time for a reality check. We struggle with inviting familiar faces into our homes, let alone strangers. Whether it's time, training, or the almighty buck, inviting people in poses challenges.

The prospect of hosting strangers compounds those challenges. It imposes on our comfort, schedule, and security. Will this stranger hurt me? What will she think of my house? Can I afford to take extra time for this person?

How can we show hospitality to people we don't know when we struggle entertaining people we know and like?

The beauty of fearing God is it casts out every other fear. Since God commands us to invite strangers in, it seems I ought to be more concerned about what may happen if I don't. It also means that if I do what He tells me, it's on Him to protect and provide for me. God always supplies the ability and resources we need to do the jobs He gives us. Focusing on our inability cripples us. How does God get the glory if we depend on our strength and resources? Bravery is choosing the better fear—fearing long-term loss over short-term pain, like exercising. Fear God. Not people. Let's focus on His power to do through us the good works He calls us to—even when it feels scary. And one of those works is showing hospitality, like brave Mrs. Grant.

---

1. W. A. Elwell and B. J. Beitzel, Baker Encyclopedia of the Bible (Grand Rapids, MI: Baker Book House, 1988), 1006.

Returning to Ruth's

She ushered me into her tiny kitchen and took the kettle off the burner. The sputtering ceased. My chilled hands and face welcomed the warmth of this steamy room. She offered me a chair. Ahhh, off my feet at last—with someone serving *me*.

"I'm Ruth, Ruth Grant. And you are?"

"Teri Donaldson. I live upstairs in twenty-one."

"Oh, up and over then. Thank you for letting me know my kettle was boiling. My ears don't work so well anymore. So, were you coming or going?"

As we conversed, Ruth reached up in the cupboard and took down two cups and saucers. From a canister on her counter, she pulled out two tea bags. The cups clinked as she placed them on the saucers and dropped tea bags in both cups.

"I was coming home from work. I do hair at Marty's."

"Where is that salon?"

"It's on Tacoma Avenue, across the street from the Harvester Restaurant."

She picked up the saucers loaded with cups and tea bags. In a slow but deliberate motion, she turned and carried them to the table. I never heard the china rattle as she moved. Though veins like ivy vines popped up under thin skin, her hands appeared strong and steady. She set the cups on the table.

"You look a bit wet. Is it raining hard?" She turned again to retrieve the kettle and poured the hot water into the cups, then returned it to the stove.

"No, just the usual drizzle. I walk to and from work."

A drawer squeaked as she drew it open to get spoons.

"That's a nice walk. About a mile, isn't it?" She opened the cupboard again, bringing down a plate. "I bet you could use a snack after walking in the rain."

She reached into her pantry and brought out a tin of shortbread. She popped off the lid. One by one, she arranged the treats on the plate. After returning to the table with spoons and cookies, she lowered herself into the chair across from me. She removed the bag from her cup. "Sugar?" she offered, motioning toward the crystal bowl in the center of the table.

"Thanks." I reached out to get a spoonful.

"Seems to me, Teri, you like your tea strong enough to get up and walk away on its own."

My teabag still steeping, I smiled. "I do. Just how I like a man. Tea and men are best when strong."

"Oh, do you have a man in your life?"

"Not yet, but when I do, he'll be strong. He'll have to be to put up with me."

We giggled.

"I understand that." Ruth chuckled. "As a career woman, my family thought I was a lost cause. My mother had given up hope that I'd ever get married and give her grandchildren."

I picked up a cookie as she spoke, enjoying its buttery sweetness and Ruth's company. That was the first of many cups of tea we shared. I discovered the same woman that Stan found annoying to be a delightful and captivating hostess.

Choose to Be Prepared

Ruth didn't plan for me to come to her door, but that didn't mean she wasn't prepared to show hospitality. A kettle is easily refilled. In her pantry, she kept treats to share.

Since God instructs us to show hospitality, trust me, He will provide us with opportunities to obey. But how prepared are we to receive strangers? Our reception of strangers reflects how we receive God.

Listen as Christ explains it in Matthew 25:35–46 (ESV):

"For I was hungry and you gave me food, I was thirsty and you gave me drink, I was a stranger and you welcomed me . . . Then the righteous will answer him, saying, 'Lord, when did we see you hungry and feed you, or thirsty and give you drink? And when did we see you a stranger and welcome you, or naked and clothe you?' . . . And the King will answer them, 'Truly, I say to you, as you did it to one of the least of these my brothers, you did it to me.'

"Then he will say to those on his left, 'Depart from me, you cursed, into the eternal fire prepared for the devil and his angels. For I was hungry and you gave me no food, I was thirsty and you gave me no drink, I was a stranger and you did not welcome me, naked and you did not clothe me, sick and in prison and you did not visit me.' Then they also will answer, saying, 'Lord, when did we see you hungry or thirsty or a stranger or naked or sick or in prison, and did not minister to you?' Then he will answer them, saying, 'Truly, I say to you, as you did not do it to one of the least of these, you did not do it to me.' And these will go away into eternal punishment, but the righteous into eternal life."

Notice the first three things Jesus listed are the essential elements of hospitality: drink, food, and shelter. It needn't be extravagant: water, simple food like apple slices or cheese, and an empty chair in our home, maybe even on the porch. It's not about preparing to *wow* people. Working to impress others inflates our egos. Unpretentious hospitality humbly serves others. It meets, greets, and seats strangers. Hospitality shares what's available and cares about others. It's about loving Jesus by loving those He sends us.

Ruth's radiance resulted, in part, from her preparation. A lack of preparation leaves us flustered and hurried. We get agitated and focus on the stuff we lack rather than the company present. Remember when Mary and Martha invited Jesus to their home? If you're unfamiliar with this story, you can find it in Luke 10:38 – 42.

Sometimes I don't prepare as well as I should. I scramble to clear clutter at the last minute and snap orders at my family. I curse under my breath about what I'm missing, the thing I can't find. But what I'm *really* missing? The one thing, the better part that Mary chose. I need to hear His whisper in my heart, "Teri, Teri, you are worried and troubled about many things. Focus on Me. I'm sitting with you even now." In those moments, I need to take a deep breath, confess my ugliness, and ask that God would cover me in the gentleness of His Son. Ruth Grant exhibited that pleasant calm as she served.

Choose to Find Friends

My great-aunt Alba showed us how friendliness looks. Ruth's example underscores the importance of making new friends. Friendships camp on common ground. Listen to your guests, as Ruth listened to me. She immediately made the connection between our professions but didn't interrupt my question to bring it up. She let me ask about her family and tell her more about myself, then politely returned to the similarity between us. If we listen to others and draw them out in conversation, finding a small plot of common ground doesn't take long. Then on that little plot of commonality, a skilled hostess erects a tent of friendship.

Abraham knew about dwelling in a tent and hospitality. In the eighteenth chapter of Genesis, we find Abraham rushing from his tent to greet three visitors, angels unaware. He quenched their thirst and nourished their bodies while engaging them in conversation.

God visited Abraham on at least five previous occasions. Through those meetings, they established a rapport. This time God shows up with two strangers. These unexpected guests revealed Abraham's amiable disposition. An intimate conversation follows their supper as God discloses His impending judgment of the cities on the plains. That revelation incites passionate intercession from Abraham, who implores God to spare his nephew, Lot. Can you see why God declares this humble host His friend in Isaiah 41:8?

I enjoy meeting people and inviting them in. At age six, I decided to throw a Halloween party—that day, after school, in *May*. I invited about a dozen classmates without ever asking my mom. My poor mom took the brunt of my spontaneous nature. She received a dozen calls from angry mothers who, unlike her, did not put used costumes in a dress-up box. My mom decided to encourage my initiative and assured the mothers there was indeed a party, and we had plenty of costumes to share. I think she served Kool-Aid, which we always had on hand, and some Chips Ahoy cookies.

Despite my ease in inviting strangers in, I struggle with a runaway tongue. It's hard work to listen and not contemplate my next comment. My impulsive interrupting of others turns guests into an audience and dialogue into a monologue. This rudeness reflects my pride, not the love of Jesus. My plan to grow grand includes learning to speak less and listen more.

Some of you feel my pain; to those who have well-disciplined tongues—we are a pain. For those who are quieter growing grand in this realm means speaking up to extend an invitation. For us clutter bums, we must choose a seating area and de-clutter it each morning. We all need a plan to be prepared. Choosing friendliness and preparedness is a good start to growing into a grand hostess, but those choices will not become habitual without this next quality I observed in Ruth.

Back to Tacoma

A few weeks later, I came home around midnight after a night out with friends. To my surprise, piano music filled the foyer. It came from Ruth's apartment. WOW! That woman can jam! The music resonated in the way only a live performance can. I stopped on the stairs just to listen. My foot tapped, keeping time with the big band jive. Closing my eyes, I could imagine her sitting at the old upright in her powder blue robe, her head bopping in time as her nimble fingers wailed on the keys. So, she was very musical, and she performed midnight concerts for her private entertainment, or so she thought. That night I listened along with her, a fabulous encore to a fun evening out!

The next day, I rapped on Ruth's door sometime in the afternoon.

She opened it, "Hi Teri. What can I do for you?"

"Do you have time for a visit?"

"Sure, come on in. Have a seat on the sofa, and I'll put the kettle on."

"I heard you playing piano last night,"

She popped her head out of the kitchen and said, "Oh, I'm sorry, was it too loud? I hope it didn't keep you up."

"No need for an apology. I didn't get in until midnight, and you only played for a few minutes afterward. I sat on the stairs just to hear you finish playing. I came by to thank you for the lovely concert."

"You should have come in," she responded. "I'm usually up to well after midnight. Just don't ever come to my door before nine in the morning. I sleep in."

Eureka, another commonality! Ruth's preference to be up late relieved me of feeling guilty about my nocturnal tendencies. Her freedom to be herself set me free too. I had always assumed old people got up early and were suspect of the work ethic of those who did not. Ruth dispelled that myth for me.

As the years pass, I've come to believe God gave people work to do twenty-four seven and wired us for different shifts. I made up a few quips on the subject, and with each one, my memory flashes back to the lively musician who inspired the following:

The early birds can have worms. Night owls eat rabbits.

Morning is for people who don't finish their work the night before.

Ooops, night owl on a rabbit trail. The discussion of her piano playing brought another helpful lesson.

"I didn't want to interrupt your recital. You play well. I enjoyed listening."

"I practice most days but not usually that late because I know some people are trying to sleep. But last night, I just got the bug, a jitterbug, and had to get it out. I'm a fair pianist, but I wish you could've heard my mom. She had talent. She taught piano for years. Even took on a charity case—me, the nonpaying student." Ruth winked, "She was clever in getting me to practice. Want to know how she did it?"

"Sure," then I heard the kettle whistle, "Oh, the water's ready,"

We headed to the kitchen for tea. Ruth continued the conversation, "When I was a child, after our supper, my mother would make me an offer, 'Ruth, would you like to go practice piano?' If my response was no, she'd go to the piano. And as she began to play, she'd say, 'Okay, then wash the dishes while I practice.' It only took a time or two to make me choose the piano."

Choose to Practice

The beauty of Ruth's mother's approach was that it caused Ruth to form a good habit of choosing to practice. Remember, our pursuit of growing grand involves developing habits of choosing well. It would be absurd to think that Ruth came into the world as a skilled musician without instruction or practice. It's no less ridiculous to believe Ruth Grant, at ninety-one, invited a stranger in for the first time. Let alone having the ability to do so in such a gracious manner. Like her piano playing, her skill as a hostess resulted from much practice.

Practice develops proficiency; disciplined, deliberate, routine practice. We have to work at hospitality if we hope to be grand at it. We must invite strangers into our homes. Then do it over and over until the habit of choosing to ask a new person into our home becomes a natural response. Practice develops that skill. Yet, the technical part of hospitality is not all we learn from Ruth. Hospitality, like her piano playing, was not a burden to her. Effortless performances result from hard work; that's when work becomes play.

God's Word not only demands hospitality, but it also directs how we should do it. "Show hospitality to one another without grumbling" (1 Peter 4:9). Do we take pleasure in serving others? Is hospitality a burden or a blessing? We must practice telling ourselves this truth: hospitality blesses Jesus, others, and us. Like the old children's song, "Jesus and others and you, what a wonderful way to spell joy. J is for Jesus, for he has first place. O is for others we meet face to face. Y is for you in whatever you do. Put yourself last and spell joy." Joy stokes a radiant countenance.

If we desire Ruth's radiance, our cheeks need the daily pushups of smiling. The cheapest and most effective facelift is a smile.

Some of us may need a little surgery and wear one more often. The practice of smiling creates the habit of choosing to smile and forms pleasant lines on our faces. I remember the first time I looked in the mirror and found I had drawn an ugly line on my face. I was only thirty-something. As I started to apply my make-up, I noticed a deep wrinkle between my eyebrows. Seeing that crack on my face shook me up. What earthquake of emotion caused that?! I started making faces to find the culprit. I discovered it came from furrowing my brows—the angry mom look—that I used to get my children's attention. Apparently, I made that face too often. It was becoming permanent. *Yikes!* I certainly didn't want to look angry for the rest of my life. I started to choose a softer look when I needed to deal with my kids. I also began massaging and stretching the line. Its shadow remains, but the deep crack is fading. I also chose to smile on purpose. So, what if I don't feel that happy? At least the smile draws lines where I want them to be. And it makes others smile when they see me smile. Try it! Smile at someone and watch their cheeks turn up.

It is said that Abraham Lincoln, when he was President of the United States, was advised to include a certain man in his Cabinet. When he refused, he was asked why he would not accept him.

"I don't like his face," the President replied.

"But the poor man isn't responsible for his face," responded his advocate.

"Every man over forty is responsible for his face," countered Abraham Lincoln.

—E.G. Manby

We think nothing of spending money on moisturizers to slow down the wrinkling of our faces, but like death and taxes, we can't avoid wrinkles. So, let's be proactive and choose habits of facial expression that lay those lines in pleasant places. Then in a few decades from now, should the Lord tarry, our faces will be radiant, like Ruth.

Radiant Ruth's Finale

Several months after our first meeting, I dropped in on Ruth and found her living room cluttered with cards. About a dozen cards decorated the room, scattered on end tables, the coffee table, and the fireplace mantel. She noticed me eying all the cards, "I just celebrated my ninety-second birthday a couple of days ago."

"Happy belated birthday! You should have told me. I would have baked you a cake."

"No need to bother. It's just another day. I went to my daughter's home for a family dinner. Four generations of us. We had a swell time!"

She enjoyed the company, but Ruth was no braggart. That was the first I knew of her age. Then she retrieved her favorite card and handed it to me. On the front of the card, I read this quote from Mark Twain, "Age is a matter of mind. If you don't mind, it doesn't matter."

"That's true, you know," she told me.

Choose to Build a Bridge in Time

With seventy-three years between us, Ruth built a bridge, not a barrier, and led me to a deeper understanding of the world around me. Ruth's friendship served as a time machine transporting me to glimpses of the past. Ruth Grant showed me the timeless beauty of a radiant countenance. Unlike the beauty of youth that fades, a lovely disposition can grow brighter over time. It doesn't grumble when the doorbell rings. It serves without complaint. A pleasant countenance opens its heart and door to a new face. This radiance is timeless because it embraces Mark Twain's sentiment and doesn't mind its age.

I learned so much from Ruth. From her insights on parenting and incredible history lessons, I grew to appreciate the value of having an elderly friend. Ruth dispelled my stereotypes of women from her era. She was a woman ahead of her time. On my buffet sits an ornate serving set; a porcelain insulated pitcher, two goblets, and a tray, all made of cast metal. It functioned as a tool for sharing cold water with those traveling the wagon trails in the late 1800s. This family heirloom, a wedding gift to my great-great-grandmother, reminds me of Ruth. Her family moved from the Midwest to Tacoma, Washington, in a covered wagon. I sometimes wonder if Ruth, as a child, had been greeted by strangers along the way. Had she ever received a drink from a pitcher and goblet like mine? No doubt, these experiences shaped her ability to show hospitality.

It is likely that as women, we will outlive our spouses. Like Ruth, we may survive many of our friends. Will we open our doors to new and younger friends? Age can build either a barrier or a bridge to new friendships. What will we build? Will the look on our faces draw people in or turn them away? An open door alone is no invitation. The countenance of the one who opens it unlocks the power of invitation. Let's choose to be brave. Let's choose to be friendly. Let's choose to be prepared and practice. Let's choose to build bridges in time. Let's open our hearts to those around us. Let's develop a radiance that draws others into our open door.

In the book of Revelation, we find Jesus knocking on our door. He wants us to host him. This challenge comes to lukewarm believers. God finds their faith neither refreshing nor soothing (the implication of "cold" and "hot" in Revelation 3:14–20). The tepid faith of lukewarm believers provokes God's rejection. I recoil at the thought of God spitting me out. I long for His fellowship. Let's remember next time the doorbell rings, it's Jesus in disguise. "Then the righteous will answer Him, saying, 'Lord, when did we see *You* hungry and feed *You*, or thirsty and give *You* drink? When did we see *You* a stranger and take *You* in . . . ? And the King will answer and say to them, 'Assuredly, I say to you, in as much as you did it to one of the least of these My brethren, you did it to *Me*,'"(Matthew 25: 37–40).

Choice Meditations

    1. Read the following three passages: Acts 10, Acts 12:5–17 (note verse 12), and Acts 16:13–15.

    2. In each passage, who showed hospitality, and how did their hospitality advance the growth of the first-century church?

    3. How can our hospitality grow the twenty-first-century church?

Choice Considerations

1. How often do you invite people over?

2. Do you invite strangers in? How often?

3. What keeps you from having people over; time, the condition of your home, money? (Remember, water is close to free.)

4. Are you praying for help to overcome these barriers?

5. Are you learning to be a good listener?

6. Look in the mirror. Where are the lines on your face? Do you need to do a little rearranging and smile more?

Choice Actions

1. Tidy up the living room. Make sure there are always two free seats. Pick a time to tidy up that space each morning so you are ready to receive unexpected guests. Then smile the whole time you do it.

2. My friend Carol learned this habit from her grandma. Make a batch of cookie dough. Freeze cookies size pieces. Smile while you work. Next time someone drops by, pull

out a few and bake cookies for your guest.

3. Next time a workman comes to your home, greet him with a big smile, thank him for coming and offer him something to drink, maybe even bake a couple more of your frozen cookie dough balls.

4. This Sunday, look for an unfamiliar face at church. With a smile, invite that person to join you for lunch after church. Keep the food simple. Focus on the guest. If you can afford it, you could take them to a restaurant.

5. Invite a neighbor you don't know into your home for a snack. Remember, smile!

6. Serve the neighborhood kids lemonade and a smile in your front yard. Learn their names and ages.

7. Next time a salesperson comes to your door, smile and offer them a glass of water.

8. Invite a woman 20–30 years your junior and another 20–30 years older than you to your home for lunch—practice bridge-building between generations. Smile, or better yet, laugh out loud together.

9. After your next guest leaves, write down three things you remember them telling you.

10

Lively Louise

Living as Long as You're Alive

Therefore, we do not lose heart. Even though our outward man is perishing, yet the inward man is being renewed day by day.
2 Corinthians 4:16

"Do you need some plants for your yard?" Cindy asked as we chatted on the phone.

"What do you have?" I wondered.

"I can bring you some lilac shoots if you'd like."

"Oh, that would be wonderful! I love lilacs, and I don't have one yet."

"Great! I'll dig some up and bring them to you when we're in Seattle."

The God Who makes all things new had led Cindy and me to new homes, yards, and churches. After a dozen years of loving our church family in Madison, Wisconsin, Bill and I returned to the Pacific Northwest, where a church in the Portland, Oregon, metro area called him to be their pastor. Cindy moved to southern Oregon the year before. We were delighted with the prospect of renewing our friendship. We moved in January. In June of the same year, our church's association's annual conference was held in Seattle. Many of our friends from my husband's seminary days also pastored churches in the fellowship. Cindy was among these old friends. Attending this event was the frosting on the cake of our move.

Cindy and I followed parallel tracks in our journeys. Her husband graduated a year before mine, and they went to his first church in Iowa. After Bill graduated, we went to Iowa for a year and then up to Wisconsin just three hours north. Cindy and Gary had returned to the Northwest before us. They planned to come to Seattle for the conference too.

I was so excited to reconnect with Cindy. We had a great visit, and true to her word, she brought me some lilac shoots, which I planted—then transplanted. Then I watched it get mowed down with a lawnmower. More on that later.

There were many delightful encounters at that conference. And it wasn't just Cindy who left me with a plant. Another woman I had not seen in over a decade planted the seed of inspiration for this book in my heart.

A Life-Giver

That year's national General Association of Regular Baptist Churches conference provided a great program. Jason Nightingale, the founder of Word Sower Ministries, recited the entire book of Romans. Ken Hamm, founder of Answers in Genesis, gave an inspiring lesson on the myth of racial segregation and the reality of one human race. The keynote speakers challenged us, the worship music engaged us, and the workshops offered met relevant needs. One, in particular, transformed my view of aging. I don't remember the workshop title. I just remember seeing the name Louise Scholes on the program. Louise Scholes! That's the workshop for me!

The small room buzzed as people found seats and visited. I looked around but saw no familiar faces. The room was packed. At this workshop for women, I noticed several men chose to join us. The presenter's reputation undoubtedly compelled them to brave this sea of estrogen.

It had been many years since I last heard Louise teach. Sitting in the workshop that day, I still remembered the outline and object lessons she used twelve years prior. Louise had a memorable way of communicating God's truth. I would not have missed that workshop for anything.

The room grew still, voices hushed. A spry woman with jet-black hair advanced to the podium. Louise stood just a bit more than five feet tall. She sported a nicely tailored, navy blue suit (skirt and blazer) with a white blouse—a classic, commanding look.

I don't remember her message that day verbatim, but here are a few unforgettable comments.

"Keep serving in your local church," encouraged Louise. "As believers, we never get to retire from serving the Lord. I turned 82 this year, and do you know what my ministry is? I work with the youth in my church. I chaperone every event they go on. Where they go, I go. They ride the bus; I ride the bus. They go skating; I go skating. When those kids need a listening ear and sound advice, guess who's there to give it? That's right, me!"

With every eye fixed on our speaker, we sat captivated.

"I want to live as long as I'm alive!" Louise declared. God planted those words—the seed of this book—in my heart. We never know how God will use our words. I'm sure Louise has no idea her example inspired a book that day—but it did.

Louise continued, "I know a lot of Christians who've died, and they're just sitting around waiting to be buried. Some of them are only in their forties!" We laughed.

That day Louise compelled us to reflect. Together we laughed, pondered, and even shed a tear or two. Louise understood the importance of staying in the fray. Like a good soldier, she refused to retreat. Not only did Louise continue the Kingdom fight, but she volunteered for the frontlines. She could have led a seniors' Bible study with her peers, but no, she marched forward to equip the next generation of church leadership. Her reputation as a Bible teacher and faithful involvement in her local church landed her on a national platform that day. A platform she used to exalt the God of life and exhort His people to come alive.

Choose to be Relevant

Rel·e·vant *adjective:* closely connected or appropriate to what is being done or considered. Synonyms: germane, appropriate, connected.

In the thirty-plus years my husband's done pastoral ministry, my observation isn't much different than Louise's. Too many followers of Christ get a "Been there. Done that. Got the t-shirt" attitude about ministry. They're content to sit on the sidelines, watching the younger folks do all the work. Newsflash: those sidelines are reserved for the saints in glory, those whose bodies lay buried (Hebrews 12:1–2). We need to grow and have a "live as long as I'm alive!" attitude if we want to be grand like Louise. The church needs the perspective and experience of her senior saints. Like the sons of Issachar who showed up to turn Saul's kingdom over to David, the true king, we need to be relevant. The Bible describes these valiant men as those "who had an understanding of the times, to know what Israel ought to do" (1 Chronicles 12:32). That's relevant! Are we engaged in our King's work? Do we have an understanding of the times? Do we know what the church ought to be doing? Are we leading the charge to bring in God's Kingdom?

Age does not render us irrelevant. Lack of involvement does. When we choose to be unaware of what's happening in the world around us, we become irrelevant. When we consider changing trends in fashion, music, and culture in general as bad because, in our flesh, we resist change, we become irrelevant. I know cultural evolution can be harmful. Sin is a shame to any generation, but not all new trends are sinful. Just because we don't care for a particular style doesn't mean it's a sin. Do we want to be in a grey-haired, dying church, singing the songs we like, sporting our threads (clothing) and dos (hairstyles) from the decade we came of age (like my idioms threads and dos), or do we want to be a part of a body that's full of all generations? Will we die holding tight to our traditionalism, or will we pass the baton of truth to young people?

There's nothing wrong with good traditions. The problem comes when we value those traditions more than God's clear commands. Christ rebuked the Pharisees for doing just that. I love how Jaroslav Pelikan puts it: "Tradition is the living faith of the dead; traditionalism is the dead faith of the living."

We must learn not only to live with younger generations but to embrace them *and* appeal to them. Choosing to be relevant means we connect with people. We get out of the house, leave our comfort zones, and *live* in the land of the living. Alone in our closets may be a great place to pray, but like King David, we will lose hope unless we believe we will see "the goodness of the Lord in the land of the living" (Psalm 27:13).

Caleb and Joshua learned to live with the next generation. Every single one of their peers died in the wilderness because they refused to follow God by faith. The fear of giants kept that first generation that had left Egypt from enjoying rest in the Promised Land. Only Caleb and Joshua remained. They had to live with and lead youngsters, a generation ignorant of the pain of slavery.

Caleb and Joshua led freeborn children in a costly battle to win a promised home. Are we willing to fight shoulder-to-shoulder with young whipper-snappers to help secure God's promises, or will we perish in a spiritual wilderness of old hymns and yesterday's testimonies? I don't know about you, but when it comes to the challenge of living with a younger generation, I'm with Caleb: "Give me this mountain!" (Joshua 14:12).

There are always giants in the Promised Land. The world's values oppose Biblical truth and embolden sinners to glory in their sins. Will we fear or face our foe? All believers fight a spiritual battle to gain ground from the enemy and rescue souls by bringing them into the Kingdom. The first time I heard Louise teach, that's what was on her heart.

A Word Sower

The wives of students attending Northwest Baptist Seminary gathered monthly to receive godly teaching from an experienced pastor or pastor's wife. After marrying Bill, I joined the group in his third year of seminary. One evening Louise Scholes was to be our speaker. She and her husband had spent many years in pastoral ministry. My husband had enrolled in a module that Harold Scholes was currently teaching. Bill encouraged me earlier in the day, "I'm glad you're going tonight. I hear Louise is a great teacher."

The walls in our meeting room at the seminary took on the rosiness of the sunset. Once settled at our desks, the wife of the seminary's president introduced Louise. Outside, a fine, spring evening faded into darkness. Inside, the sunshine burned brightly as Louise opened her Bible and began to pull items from a plain, brown paper bag one by one. I found myself drawn to her message by her down-to-earth manner. She kept us engaged with awe and laughter as she taught the passage of scripture. Ten years later, I could recite each item she used and each point she made. Unfortunately, thirty years later, I only remember one. The last one. The most important one.

She had spoken about a Bible passage about sharing the Gospel. The last Item drawn from her bag was a ladle. "To share the gospel, you need a long dipper. You need it so you can reach down into your heart. If you're not actively sharing Jesus, you need to get way down in your heart and ask yourself why. Use that dipper to get out all of your excuses. The lost need to hear the Gospel, and we need to get rid of any excuse we have for not sharing it with them."

Now that's how we slay giants, ladies, with the sword which is the word of God (Ephesians 6:17). To "live as long as I'm alive," I need to be a lifelong student of God's word. This "sword that makes the wounded whole" (as Keith Getty calls it in his song *Oh, Church Arise*) changes us if we let it. Too often, I'm tempted to make lazy excuses like, "That's just how I am." In trying to preserve who I've been, I will lose the opportunity to become who I should be. I'll choose to remember that while God gives me breath, He has a purpose for my life. That purpose serves as a better chauffeur than my feelings. My feelings will drive me crazy. Purpose drives me where God will use me.

Choose to Teach Good Things

God makes our purpose clear.

"But as for you, speak the things which are proper for sound doctrine: . . . the older women likewise, that they are reverent in behavior, not slanderers, not given to much wine, *teachers of good things*—that they admonish the young women to love their husbands, to love their children, to be discreet, chaste, homemakers, good, obedient to their own husbands, that the word of God may not be blasphemed" (Titus 2:1–5 italics added for emphasis).

Teaching God's word is not a job reserved for those women who have the gift of teaching. God commissions all qualified older women to instruct the younger ones. We teach by our examples, but teaching doesn't stop with our modeling.

God calls on us to use words to teach about the subjects of integrity and family relationships. We must teach His Word so younger women can live out His Word. To what end? So that His Word is not blasphemed. This high and holy calling serves as all the purpose you and I will ever need to "live as long as we're alive." This is disciple-making—showing younger women how to walk with Christ. But making disciples requires more than just involvement with fellow believers.

The Great Commission commands we "go into all the world." We need to go to unbelievers; we need to teach disciples *and* make disciples by sharing the good news, the gospel. Get out that "long dipper," ladies. Are you going? If not—why not?

My husband and I have served three different churches; two small (under 150) and the current one much larger (about 500). After my first year in our present church ministry, I realized I could have quite a full social calendar without ever meeting an unsaved soul. I knew I needed to go out of my church doors if I was going to fulfill my God-given purpose of sharing the gospel. So, I went back to work part-time.

The store I work at is my mission field. I've had the opportunity to share my conversion story with two Muslim men and several women. I do it on breaks when casual conversation allows me that freedom. To be God's faithful ambassador, I must respect company policy and not rob my employer's time. I revere God by respecting my boss. You may already be in the workplace. Do you consider it your mission field? "Look, I tell you, lift up your eyes, and see that the fields are white for harvest," Jesus said (John 4:35). Do you pray for coworkers? How about praying *with* them? Are you sharing God's word with them as opportunities arise?

Once at work, I prayed with two women because they refused to get along. One was a Jehovah's Witness. The other woman told everyone that her grandpa was a pastor but lived a life that didn't reflect Christian values. Their dislike of each other polluted the work environment. Gossip and complaints spewed out of their mouth like sewage into an open waterway. So, when no customers were around, I took them aside. "Both of you claim to follow God. Jesus commands us to love each other. The way you treat each other is *not* loving! And we're going to pray about it right now." And I prayed. I prayed the Prince of Peace would enter their lives and teach them to be at peace with each other.

God honored that prayer. Neither of these women complained about me to management, and they began treating each other better. Was either of these women born again? I don't know. I do know I did what God wanted me to do by inviting these women into a relationship with Him.

We can go in many ways: volunteer, get involved in community service, pray as we walk through our neighborhoods, and invite neighbors to a Bible study. That's what my good friends Susie and Carmen did. They now meet weekly with two neighbors and study the Gospel of Luke with these women. I hope you are actively involved in the lives of people who do not follow Jesus. If you're not, use that long dipper stick to figure out what's hindering you, and go!

Louise's Lasting Impression

That evening in a classroom at Northwest Baptist Seminary, I imprinted on Louise Scholes like a newly hatched chick. I already loved God and His Word, but that night, I fell in love with teaching. I wanted to grow up in my faith, teach the Bible, and share my faith just like Louise. I longed to ignite the hearts of young women the way Louise ignited mine. It's been said people only need three things in life, someone to love, something to do, and something to look forward to. The Creator of the universe provides us with all three: we have Him and those he died to save to love, we have the work of making disciples to do, and Heaven to look forward to. And the more years we've lived, the more our bodies decline, the better Heaven looks. Life is exhausting. Heaven is rest!

Heaven restores relationships with God and our brothers and sisters in Christ. I miss Louise and Cindy. I'll never forget their gifts. That brings us back to the lilac shoot Cindy brought me. That poor bush suffered all kinds of trauma, but today, that bush stands eight feet tall. Every spring, it blooms full of fragrant, lavender flowers. Grand women are a lot like lilac bushes. They get cut down and uprooted, but they keep growing more robust and beautiful as the years accumulate. I need Louise's reminder to grow that way, inwardly "renewed day by day" (2 Corinthians 4:16).

Above the island in my kitchen hangs a holder for pots, pans, and kitchen utensils; a large ladle dangles from one of the hooks. That "long dipper" takes me back to an object lesson taken out of a brown paper bag. It begs these questions, "Are you relevant? Are you sharing and teaching good things from God's word?" Thanks to Louise, I received this baton of Truth. Her example as a woman of valor still challenges me to be a good soldier, like the sons of Issachar. And just like Louise, I, too, want to live as long as I'm alive!

Choice Meditations

1. In John 10:7–10, for what purpose did Jesus tell us He came? Describe what abundant looks like to you. If you have access to a Strong's Concordance (or another Greek lexicon), use the Greek lexicon and discover the fuller meaning of this word translated "abundantly" in John 10:10.

2. Read John 11:17–27, then consider Romans 6:4. Is the resurrection just a future hope? If not, what implication does it have for your life today?

3. Review the context of Romans 6:4. Read Romans 6:1–6 and Psalm 51:1–13. What robs us of joy and newness of life? What restores it?

Choice Considerations

1. How does your life compare to your understanding of abundant life (consider what you learned in the previous section)? What sin may be hindering the abundance of your life?

2. Reflect on this statement: "It's been said people only need three things in life, someone to love, something to do, and something to look forward to." How do you agree or disagree with this thought? Write a list using this statement

as three separate headings. First, list those with whom you enjoy a loving relationship. Secondly, what do you have to do? List jobs, hobbies, and goals. Last, what are you looking forward to both here and in eternity?

3. How are you intentionally following the instruction given to older women in Titus 2:3–5?

Choice Actions

1. After considering what you were already doing to comply with Titus 2:3–5, think of one more thing you can do to live out these instructions and do it.

2. Before you get out of bed, take a moment to praise God for who He is, and thank Him for the day He's giving you and the work He provides for you to do.

3. Daily watch or read the news if you don't already. Pray about what's going on in the world.

4. Thumb through a fashion magazine once in a while. Go shopping with a much younger friend and have her help you pick an item or two to update your wardrobe. This shopping trip could double as mentoring time. She can school you on fashion, and you can teach her about the weightier matters of living.

5. Savor the moments of the day. Smell your food before you gobble it down, and enjoy the aroma. Listen to the birds out your window or children playing in the neighborhood. Stop and smell the roses, for real. Take pleasure in being

alive, and enjoy the abundance of beauty God has created all around you. Live as long as you're alive!

11

Courageous Chloris

Living Victoriously

*"But we have this treasure in earthen vessels, that the excellence
of the power may be of God and not of us. . .always carrying about
in the body the dying of the Lord Jesus, that the life of Jesus also
may be manifested in our body."*
2 Corinthians 4:7, 10

The smell of sweet grapes filled Chloris's steamy kitchen.
She held the cheesecloth bag over a large pot as I poured
the warm, stewed fruit through it. Pouring out the stockpot was
easy (for me)—my arms were young and robust. Then I watched
in amazement as Chloris twisted every drop of juice out of that
cheesecloth. Her arms were twice as old as mine, but the strength
she exhibited surprised me. She battled rheumatoid arthritis. This
ruthless disease left her hands gnarled and deformed. She thought
she was teaching me how to make jam, but she schooled me in
handling pain.

My lifelong friendship with Chloris began when the church she
and her husband had planted fell on tough times. They could no
longer support a full-time pastor. Herb and Chloris Kietzke met

my husband and me at a mission conference where Bill was one of the speakers. He shared our heart to plant a church in Madison, Wisconsin. We hoped the church throwing the conference would partner with us. It was in the neighboring town of Verona. Herb and Chloris Kietzke had once been members of this church before breaking off to start a church in Madison themselves, twenty years before. The Kietzkes invited us for dinner at their home on one day of the week-long mission event.

Chloris and Herb greeted us at the door. Their home appeared spacious and well-kept. Sitting in the living room, we enjoyed the view through the large picture windows that composed the entirety of the long back wall. The house sat on the edge of the woods; sitting inside felt like being in the forest with climate control. A large stone fireplace opened to both the living and dining rooms, separating the two spaces. It stood like a stone bluff amid their private woods. On the opposite wall in the living room stood an organ and a piano.

After seating us in the living room, Chloris disappeared into her kitchen. We could hear her pulling the roast from the oven. Herb excused himself to help lift it to the platter and help Chloris bring the hot dishes to the table. Good thing we arrived on time because the meal was ready and the table set. Punctuality was one of Chloris's many good traits.

Chloris always set a meticulous table. Fine china, her mother's depression-glass serving bowls, and well-polished silverware laid on top of crisp, white napkins. Each took its proper place on the white linen tablecloth. This meal reminded me of dining at Great-Grandma Burton's; no doubt, it was the presence of the relish tray containing sweet pickles and olives. A bygone etiquette had honed Chloris's abilities in hospitality. She greeted her guests with beauty, graciousness, and tasty food.

Throughout our conversation, we discovered many things about each other. The Kietzkes had only one son, but he and their daughter-in-law blessed them with three granddaughters. I was seven months pregnant with our first child. We shared a passion for the city of Madison.

"I'd be plowing the high part of my field, up where the water tower sits, and I'd look out across the field. I'd see new construction creeping this way. I could hear the words of Jesus, 'Like sheep without a shepherd.' Those folks would need a good church. That's when the Lord laid it on my heart to plant one. I had plenty of acres, so I dedicated a parcel to the Lord. We built a small building first, one that we could remodel to sell as a house. Later we built the one on top of the hill," Herb told us.

After dinner and dessert, we continued our conversation in the living room. Chloris explained the church's current dilemma.

"I've been church treasurer for several years. These past few years have been tough. We've had families move away, and our attendance is quite low. One day I just had to tell the pastor there's not enough in the church's checking account to pay you and the bills. I think you may need to resign. Shortly after this, the pastor decided he should resign, and we should go back to mission status and find a fully supported missionary pastor."

"That's why we've invited you. Would you consider filling the pulpit until we secure a new pastor?" Herb asked.

So Bill and I ended up in a church rescue instead of church planting. The Kietzkes donated five acres of their family farm to erect a church building. The community of saints slowly grew. By the time Bill and I came, they had managed to build an ample facility. It could seat about 130 people. This small church acted in faith. When constructing the structure, there were only around thirty in the congregation. But as churches do, attendance ebbed, and now they had only about a dozen, not enough to support a full-time pastor.

My husband planned on being a tent-making missionary by getting a full-time job to support his "preaching habit" (that's how Bill described it to his co-workers). We also knew we would need a small group, at least a dozen people willing to be in the church plant. The Kietzke's offer of a pulpit provided a small group and a building to boot. We felt blessed to receive the call for Bill to be Meadowood's pastor. They offered us a whopping seventy-five dollars a week, just enough for groceries, more than we expected if we were planting a church.

Eventually, Meadowood extended the call to Bill to become their permanent pastor. We accepted. Hence, my life with Chloris began. She was sixty-one. I was twenty-five. For twelve years, my husband served as her pastor. After leaving Meadowood, Chloris and I enjoyed keeping company through Christmas letters. On my family's annual returns to Wisconsin to visit Bill's family, we would always worship with our Meadowood family. Chloris and I also took advantage of those visits to renew our relationship. I enjoyed the privilege of knowing her for the last twenty-one years of her life.

Chloris's delicate features and elegant style resembled more a porcelain doll than a farmer's wife. Herb even called her his Dolly. Her slender frame and modest apparel hid the tawny muscles hardened by years of labor. And her quiet gentleness concealed the strength of her perseverance. The glint in her eyes spoke volumes of her sharp mind while her well-tamed tongue said little. Chloris's pleasant countenance covered much pain, both heartache and physical suffering. The deformity of her feet inflicted by RA always hid inside plain orthotic shoes, but her hands exposed the havoc wreaked by the disease. Her fingers bent down at an awkward angle from her hand; every knuckle doubled in size by swelling. Yet, she chose to be mastered by her love of music, not RA. She was Meadowood's only pianist for many years. When another church pianist came along, she switched to playing the organ. She practiced every day she could.

Music served as her physical therapist. "I've got to keep playing if I want my fingers to keep moving," she told me. And play she did. Herb had a marvelous baritone voice. They enjoyed making music together. I can still hear Herb belting out, "I'm so glad I'm a part of the family of God. . ." as Chloris wailed on the keys with as much force as she could muster.

In the twelve years I attended Meadowood, Chloris endured four reconstructive surgeries. These surgeries involved Chloris wearing reconstructive braces for several weeks. The hand brace reminded me of Edward Scissor Hands. From the wrist brace, five long metal rods extended above her fingers, with a wire on each one dropping to hold the finger below in its proper place while her hand healed. Surgery and occasional travel were the only two things I can remember that ever interrupted Chloris's piano playing.

While her physical pain was evident, her heartache was not. In the past couple of years of my own life, I have come to appreciate the disappointment Chloris endured. Not until one of my own children's marriages hit bottom could I begin to know how Chloris felt when her son and his wife divorced because of his infidelity, leaving her three precious granddaughters victims of a broken family. Sucker-punched in the gut by a call from my child's spouse, I crumpled to the floor in tears. Herb's warning given to me twenty years before echoed in my ears, "The time you spend now on all the demands of your little children will not free up when they're gone. You'll be spending that time on your knees, praying for them." He said it with moist eyes and a grieving tone.

I had expected a little sympathy, not the response Herb gave me when I told him how I looked forward to the slower pace of an empty nest. Herb was right, parenting never stops, and it can be excruciating. Chloris's heart hurt just as much as Herb's over their son's poor choices.

Despite her severe trials, Chloris chose to find joy in the reality that her Great Physician was in the process of making her better. Somehow through her pain, the God she knew and loved was working for her good—working to make her more like Jesus.

Choose not to Complain

Pain is a powerful motivator for complaining. I can't begin to tell you how often I succumb to complaining when my body hurts. Yet, in all the years I knew Chloris, I never heard her complain, not even once. Rather than letting pain master her, she chose to let the joy of the Lord be her strength. And that joy veiled her pain with a beautiful countenance. All the folks at church enjoyed spending time with her. She graced all in her presence with thoughtful conversations centered around many things, but *never* her aches and pains.

Chloris trusted that the God Who can heal was concerned with making her whole, not comfortable. Healing our hearts is far more critical than healing our bodies. Sometimes inner healing requires outward brokenness. James tells us to, "Count it all joy, my brothers, when (*not if*) you meet trials of various kinds, for you know that the testing of your faith produces steadfastness. And let steadfastness have its full effect, that you may be perfect and complete, lacking in nothing" (James 1:2-4). The Greek word translated steadfastness carries the idea of cheerful endurance. Complaining is not a pleasant choice.

If I want to benefit from difficulties, I must choose hope and stop complaining. I need to take joy in the truth that God loves me too much to leave me like I am instead of complaining about how painful the change process feels. Chloris fought her temptation to complain and won. She walked victoriously, counting it all joy. Her faith was complete; Chloris lacked nothing because she chose to cooperate with her Heavenly Father and stay cheerfully under His training for her life. Her training included the exercise of perseverance in her marriage.

Herb's Helpmeet

It's hard for me to think of Chloris apart from Herb. They were one. Not in an unhealthy co-dependent sense. They were each strong individuals but together—through 60 years of marriage—they developed a powerful synergy. Herb was the more prominent figure of this couple, more outspoken, more passionate. Yet Chloris made him better. She completed him.

Herb was a lot of things: he was a hardworking farmer, a committed follower of Christ, a strict father, and a loving grandfather, but mostly Herb was a *handful*. He was strong-willed and straightforward. You never had to guess what was on Herb's mind. "We need to sing more hymns," he told our worship leader. "People shouldn't be wearing shorts to worship on Sundays," he complained in a Wednesday night prayer meeting. Then he lamented how no one came to pray on Wednesdays anymore. Fortunately, that prayer meeting consisted of just the Keitzkes and my family. I was relieved no one else had heard Herb's disparaging comments. My husband ended the traditional midweek service a short time later and began in-home Bible studies throughout the week. Three small groups met with a total of fifty participants. Herb expressed his displeasure with the cancelation of Wednesday nights in no uncertain terms to my husband. Yup, Herb was a handful, but we didn't have to live with him. Chloris did! And she did it well.

When Herb had the vision to plant a new church in Madison, Chloris supported it wholeheartedly. Before the first building was built, she opened her home for small group Bible studies and prayer meetings. Chloris helped in both of the building projects by being a gofer. You know, go for this, go for that. She willingly left all the amenities of a large church in exchange for doing everything in a church plant. She left a few choice places of service and began doing it all because she shared Herb's vision. Chloris had the burden and also saw the need for a new church in Madison. Chloris had spent her early married years feeding Herb's hired hands and doing her share of chores to build a lucrative farm, and now, after retirement, she joined her farmer-husband in the harvest of souls for the Kingdom of God.

From the day she said "I do" until the day Herb breathed his last, she remained his faithful companion. She was his homemaker but never his doormat, a submissive partner but always his equal. She took his side when he was right, but when he was wrong, in the privacy of their home, she'd let him know. Take, for instance, the Sunday Herb chewed out my daughter and her friend.

I sat in one of the front pews with my three girls. My oldest daughter's friend, Cori, skipped over to join us. In our small church, the children often joined another family to sit with a friend. During the message, Cori began quietly braiding Rachel's hair. Cori was a spunky girl. Sitting still didn't much agree with her, and I thought she had picked an excellent way to divert her energy. Herb, however, disagreed. He and Chloris were sitting behind us. As soon as the last hymn ended, he lit into Rachel and Cori. "That was so rude of you two to be so distracting! Worship service is no place to be fixing hair! You know better than that!"

The girl's eyes, wide with fear, stared up at Herb. They stood speechless, shocked. Herb had always been so friendly, like an extra grandpa. They didn't know what to say. My shock turned quickly to anger. I had been the supervising adult who chose not to stop them. I felt Herb's beef should be with me, not the girls. Chloris was shocked too. Later in the foyer, she apologized for her husband's bad behavior.

"I told him he needed to ignore the girls. They were quiet, and he was the adult. I am so sorry. He should not have scolded them like that."

"Thanks, Chloris. I didn't think the girls were being naughty. I couldn't believe he reacted that way," I told her.

"The girls were being just fine. It's Herb who has a problem."

Her words helped cool my jets and gave me an objective view of the situation. I went home, talked it over with my husband, and prayed about what to do. I considered the instruction Jesus gave, "If your brother sins against you, go and tell him his fault, between you and him alone. If he listens to you, you have gained your brother" (Matthew 18:15). It became pretty clear what I needed to do.

I needed to go to Herb for his good and the good of the girls, who were only seven and ten years old. I wanted children to want to be in church, not frightened to be there. And I knew, deep down, Herb wanted that too. He had sinned against us, and he needed to own it and ask for forgiveness. This was going to be tough. I was half his age, his pastor's wife, and he was a charter member and deacon in the church. I needed to approach him with respect and love.

Later that day, as I sat alone with Herb, I began by asking him to open his Bible and read a selected passage. Then I patiently asked, "Herb, is that how you treated Cori and Rachel today?"

"Well, no, but they were being naughty."

"Herb, is braiding hair in church sinful?"

"Well, I guess not . . . not really," he admitted in a sheepish tone.

"So back to the Bible passage you read, is that how you treated the girls today?"

Finally, Herb realized his sinfulness. He asked the little girls for forgiveness and me for mine. However, I know I am not the only individual the Holy Spirit used to convict and humble Herb that day. Chloris had been talking to him too. She paved the way for this difficult conversation. In the end, doing the hard thing—the right thing—paid off. We restored our relationship, and the girls learned a valuable lesson. Grown-ups, even church leaders, are not always correct or kind, but godly leaders humble themselves and ask forgiveness when they sin. Chloris helped Herb be that Christ-like leader. That day, sin and fear were defeated because Chloris dared to tell her husband when he was wrong. Wrong or right, Herb was her man, and she was his "Dolly."

The two adored each other. I can still see Herb's doting expression as he thanked Chloris for the meals she made or talked about their travel together. His eyes got that boyish twinkle, and the corners of his mouth would lift in a shy, tilted grin. Chloris admired her husband's work ethic and many skills he'd developed over the years. They sang each other's praises in perfect harmony. Sometimes their praise gave way to laments of concern when the potential loss of the other threatened.

When Herb landed in the hospital after suffering a heart attack, Chloris hovered over him with all the attention of a mother bird. She'd flit quickly away to attend to a need, then return to his bedside to continue her vigil. Their hearts carried mutual concern; what would she do without him? They were confident of Herb's final destination, Heaven, but he wanted his travel partner with him. He wondered who'd care for her. With RA, there was no way for Chloris to stay in that big home alone. Chloris had always kept house and cooked for him, exchanging ideas with him, cuddled close with him in bed each night, his warmth soothing her aching joints. With Herb in the hospital facing an empty house and an empty bed, each night was hard for Chloris. How, she wondered could she do it for years? Who would she spend her days with, her energies on? Their worried faces posed a challenge for their young pastor and his wife; we couldn't understand what they were facing. Oh, Bill and I understood, in theory, that heart attacks are scary. People die. Widows and widowers are left behind. Until you've enjoyed 40 or more years of intimacy with the love of your life, you're clueless about the pain they feel. We prayed with them and listened to them pray, and watched as together they cast their cares on the One Who cared most for them. We watched them gain courage. And through this trial, they encouraged us.

Long-term marriages display three different chemistries. Oil and vinegar couples, which get shaken together, mix for a while but soon revert to two separate individuals, each content in their space. Then there's the vinegar and soda mix, explosive couples that infuriate each other. Yikes! Finally, and most rare, are sugar and hot water couples. The two become one, and they warm and sweeten the world around them as their years evaporate. That was Herb and Chloris. Oh, like any couple, they had oil and vinegar days and even some soda and vinegar days, but for the most part, their sweet oneness defined them.

I long for that subtle, romantic affection in my marriage; the exchange of coy smiles, sparkling eyes filled with delight as we gaze at one another, the reaching for a hand to hold, a gentle arm around a shoulder. I'm not talking about hormone-driven couples that can't keep their hands off each other. I have in mind the discreet affection built on a lifetime of trust and intimacy—the quiet way true lovers love in public. Though I married a man who can be hot water, he married a woman who is now more oily than sweet. But I believe there is hope. Jesus can crystalize my resolve to be a better wife, to become the sugar that dissolves into Bill's warm companionship. I can choose to be sweet and resolve to dissolve. If I succeed in my pursuit, it will be because, like Chloris, I choose to keep commitments.

Choose to be Committed

If you've been married for five years, or maybe just five days, you've discovered firsthand that happily-ever-after only exists in fairytales. The perfect Prince Charming remains a myth. Men come incomplete because God made them that way. I love the old Hebrew joke that some professors use to teach their students the Hebrew words for man and woman. "God made man and said '*Ish*' (Hebrew for man), this boy needs help. So, God made the woman, and the man said '*Isha!*' (Hebrew for woman)." It doesn't take long for wives to discover the *ish* we pledged our lives to. What takes a lifetime is to fulfill that vow and look out for his good, help him chase his dreams, and fulfill his calling. Yet that's what a courageous wife does.

It takes courage to stay in a marriage, even a good one. The world around us tells us we should put our happiness first. How often have we heard, "You shouldn't put up with him," or "He doesn't deserve you," and worst of all, "You should leave him." Divorce is the go-to when marriage gets difficult. But a courageous woman is no buttercup; she sucks it up.

Do you remember the movie, *The Princess Bride?* Princess Buttercup acted like a prima donna, and the ever-faithful farm boy who doted on her always responded to her requests with, "As you wish." While it might be nice for a day, I wouldn't want that for a lifetime. The give and take, the exchange of ideas, and embracing the same goals and dreams are what make a marriage meaningful. It takes two strong individuals to make a strong, healthy marriage. One spoiled brat, one wimpy partner, and the marriage becomes weak, a poor picture of the Triune God Who's image it should display. "The wise woman builds her house. The foolish woman tears it down with her own hands" (Proverbs 14:1). I want to choose to keep working at my marriage, to complete the man God gave me. Note, I said complete, *not* compete.

Any time you put two strong people together, they will face the temptation to compete. We need to resist that and get on the same team, be a team. I've struggled with this most recently as an empty nester. I spent most of my married life as a full-time homemaker raising kids. This was both my preference and choice. I would not have married Bill if he had not agreed to support me being at home with our children. Now I'm on to my next endeavor, writing. I feel, at times, like my ambition competes with my husband's interests. I hear myself whining, "What about my calling, my desires, my needs?" In reality, our calling is one, and my writing is just a new fulfillment of our call as a couple to make disciples. The fact is with my Z-type personality (A-types are high energy, B-types are slower pace, and Z-types would siesta all day if someone doesn't wake them up), I don't know if I could even write books if I had to work full time. I am a well-kept woman because my husband takes his role as our provider seriously and does value my contribution to our calling. Chloris and Herb modeled this mutual respect for my husband and me. Now we model it for other young married couples.

I fear this mutual respect is dying in our individualistic culture. American society generally looks down on women who don't bring in a paycheck. Young stay-at-home moms worry about spending their husbands' pay on themselves. Really, can he afford to replace you? Can he afford a weekly housekeeper, cook, childcare provider, mistress, and counselor? My husband's paycheck wouldn't go that far. Chloris and I chose to see our husbands' money as a household income. It's ours, not his or mine. Our worth as women cannot be summed up by the digits in a salary. No one is worth that *little*. Our value is not based on what we contribute. God values us as His image-bearers. That alone is the reality on which all mutual respect *should* be established. God breathes life into people. That singular act gives us each fantastic worth. Whether strong or weak, healthy or ill, capable or disabled, God designed each of us and gave us life. He values every person. To choose to keep commitments to people requires us to respect them on that premise alone.

You may be single and want to be married. You may be divorced or widowed and want another shot at holy matrimony. You may be perfectly content to stay single. All of these desires are valid. Whatever your situation, know this: courageous women keep their commitments to others—to their friends, families, churches, and even to their enemies. "Let your 'Yes' be 'yes,'" Jesus counsels (Matthew 5:37). In the previous chapter, I shared we need to choose to be women of the Word, to share and teach God's Word. To do that, we need to be women who keep our word. Loving our neighbor as ourselves takes commitment. I must choose to *value* others, *respect* them, *make time* for them. This is how marriages last, churches grow, and communities become strong. These are the fruits of commitment.

Commitment unites us and provides security. Listen to the many synonyms: obligation, pledge, charge, duty, must, need, ought, burden, requirement, and responsibility. This sense of duty has become passé. It's hard, even unpleasant at times, to be committed to other sinners, but that difficulty is the price courage is willing to pay. It's an obligation to love someone even when you don't like them.

Proverbs 31 tells about the excellent or virtuous wife, how rare and precious she is. The Hebrew word, virtuous or excellent for women, is more often used to describe men. When speaking of men, it's always translated as valor. I can never be a perfect woman. Isn't perfect what comes to mind when we think of the words virtuous and excellent? However, I can stay in the fray, be loyal, and keep my vows. I believe God calls us to do just that, to be women who don't retreat or wimp out when relationships feel like a battle. We must remain loyal to the people we've committed ourselves to: neighbors, churches, friends, families, and especially our husbands (for those of us who are married). For richer and poorer, in sickness and in health, until death do us part. That's how Chloris kept her commitments.

I once asked Chloris why she didn't teach Sunday school anymore. Without missing a beat, she replied, "Oh, I do. I teach the Pastor's wife class." She gave me a knowing smile. The day Chloris invited me over to make jam, I suspect she *did* know she was teaching me how to handle more than grapes. Her offer to pass down a life skill like jam-making allowed her to spend time keeping her commitment to me as my Sunday school teacher.

One time I visited her home, I admired her Christmas Cactus. The massive plant sprawled three feet wide; four feet long limbs hung to the floor.

"I've had it for years." Chloris told me, "Would you like some starters?"

"Sure!"

She broke off three or four pieces and tucked them in a wet paper towel. "Just plant these in a pot when you get home. Make sure you keep them well watered until the roots get started," she told me.

So, I did. Now almost three decades later, I have a lovely Christmas cactus about the same size as the one it started from. Through the years, the base of the main limbs has grown thick, taking on a rough bark-like appearance. It reminds me of Chloris's gnarled joints. It's showing its age. However, age hasn't stopped it from growing and blooming. Twice a year, it cascades with bright fuchsia flowers as vibrant and beautiful as Chloris. I planted a few clippings from her plant in a pot. God planted her example in my heart. If I choose not to complain and keep committed, my life will bloom with vibrant beauty like Chloris's.

Choice Meditations

1. Read Philippians 2:12–18. In the first two verses, what work are we called to do? What work is God doing?

2. How do those observations help you understand Paul's command in Philippians 2:14?

3.

What motivation does Paul give us to obey the command? In other words, what results from our obedience?

4. In Philippians 2:17, how does Paul describe his ministry? Read Mark 14:3–9. What was broken and poured out and by whom? Describe how Jesus was broken and poured out. How do these examples encourage you to be broken and poured out without complaint?

5. Read Matthew 5:33–37. What do you learn about keeping your word from this passage?

Choice Considerations

1. Do you enjoy being with someone who complains? Listen to yourself this week. How much are you complaining out loud? In your heart?

2. When you cry out to the Lord in the complaint, are you asking for wisdom, strength, and His will to be done, or do you simply crave relief?

3. Do you think of serving others as a burden or a privilege?

4. Would you describe how you keep commitments as sacrificial (I'll do my part even if you don't do yours) or reciprocal (if you do your part, I'll do mine)?

5. How carefully do you make commitments? Are you keeping the commitments you've made?

Choice Actions

1. When you're tempted to complain about something, choose to say something positive instead. Give thanks or a compliment instead.

2. Instead of focusing on your aches and pains, ask others how you can pray for them.

3. Once a day, do something painful that you know is good for you: exercise, eat less or better (cut some sugar out), get up or go to bed earlier, and watch less TV.

4. Once a day, think about what you can do to help your spouse, roommate, or neighbor.

5. Compliment the people you live with (or closest to) every day.

6. If you don't already, pay your bills on time. Show up for work, appointments, and church on time. A great man once said punctuality is the art of wasting only your time.

7. If you must fail at keeping a commitment, be responsible enough to call and let the party involved know you'll be late or not coming. Work out a lower, longer payment schedule with creditors if you can't pay a bill.

8. Finally, choose not to complain about those who fail you. Confront them, challenge them, encourage them, but *don't* complain about them.

12

Demure Doris

Living Classy

*"Her clothing is fine linen and purple. Her husband is known
in the gates when he sits among the elders of the land. She
makes linen garments and sells them; she delivers sashes to the
merchant. Strength and dignity are her clothing, and she laughs
at the time to come."*
Proverbs 31:22b–25

"**C**an I enlist your help for some fun at the retreat this year?"
I asked Doris. "Our theme is girlfriends, and girlfriends
share secrets. So, we thought it would be fun to ask if anyone had
a tattoo and if they'd show it to us. I know you're *not* inked, but I
also know you love a good practical joke. Would you be willing to
sport a fake one? You could wash it off before you go home."

"Oh no, I'm going to wear it home and show, Loyd!" (This is not
a typo, Loyd Lowe spelled his name with one l.)

And she did!

That following Sunday, after we returned from the retreat,
Doris's husband, Loyd, pulled me aside with a stern look on his
face, "I hear you led my wife into sin. We're going to have words

about this," he told me with playful eyes betraying his amusement. He loves teasing. He enjoyed the laugh as much as the ladies at the retreat did.

Doris' demeanor appeared prim and proper. But I had it on good authority that she had been a notorious practical joker in college. A few years before this incident at Loyd and Doris Lowe's fiftieth-anniversary party, her sister-in-love shared this story with me.

"Doris was a couple of years ahead of me in Bible college. We shared the same dorm. She served as the dorm leader. One of her responsibilities was to do daily room inspections. One morning before breakfast, after everyone but she and I had left, she said, 'Come help me remake these beds.' And the two of us short-sheeted the whole dorm. I couldn't believe my lovely, mature, soon-to-be sister-in-law would be such a bad influence on me." She grinned, "It was hilarious!"

Doris understood the line of discretion, what's funny and what isn't. And she was always happy to push us to laugh and never cross the line. The pleasant lines on her face reveal Doris laughs well and often. She understands laughter's power to relax and rejuvenate. Not everyone understands this.

I remember leaving a session at a women's retreat. A friend and I walked behind a small group of older women and overheard this conversation. "What was the point of that chicken skit? It was ridiculous."

"I agree. It was completely unnecessary. There was no spiritual benefit whatsoever!"

The tone of these women sounded pious and critical. I looked at my friend; she and I chuckled. The point of the skit was simple. Just laugh! We felt sorry for these old biddies. They chose to be critics instead of receiving the blessing of comic relief. We need to laugh.

Choose to Laugh

Laughter is more than good medicine; it's the elixir of eternal youth. It's the international language of happiness. And it's the best facial we can give ourselves. Let's etch some fun lines on our faces. Go ahead, LOL! Blessed are the easily amused. They shall laugh more often.

When I plan a retreat or prepare for a speaking engagement, I pray, "Lord, please give us laughter and tears." Laughter relaxes us by releasing stress. It creates a sense of freedom and a reprieve from unpleasantness and pain. It pulls down barriers and connects us. Tears release pain. And when we cry with others, tears engender intimacy. Sharing tears and laughter creates loving friendships. My goal in ministry is to create loving relationships and help women connect with God and one another. Laughter plays a big part in that.

God laughs (Psalm 37:13), and so should we. He tells us to laugh at the appropriate time (Ecclesiastes 3:4). Do you laugh when you spend time with God? I hope so. He tells some brilliant jokes. I hope you're getting them. He uses sarcasm, wordplay, and irony better than any professional comedian. He even uses physical comedy. For example, how did He break the four hundred years of silence between the Old Covenant and the announcement of the coming Messiah? He spoke through a mute priest. Yup, Zacharias, the father of John the Baptist, got word his barren wife would have a son who would be the one to prepare Israel for her Savior. God broke the silence with silence. It was ironic and slapstick as He took away Zacharias's speaking ability. That's funny! Read it for yourself in Luke 1:5–25. And how about the time He promised to give Abraham and Sarah a son? Imagine a ninety-year-old woman pregnant.

Abraham laughed. Sarah laughed. And God had the last laugh. They named the boy Laughter (the meaning of Isaac) because, as Michael Card's ballad of this story tells us, "No other name would do."

If you're not convinced of your need to laugh yet, consider this excerpt from an article on the Mayo Clinic's website (mayoclinic.org/healthy-lifestyle/stress-management/in-depth/stress-relief/art-20044456).

Stress Relief from Laughter

A good sense of humor can't cure all ailments, but data is mounting about the positive things laughter can do.

Short-Term Benefits

A good laugh has significant short-term effects. When you start to laugh, it doesn't just lighten your load mentally; it induces physical changes in your body. Laughter can:

- **Stimulate many organs.** Laughter enhances your intake of oxygen-rich air, stimulates your heart, lungs, and muscles, and increases the endorphins released by your brain.

- **Activate and relieve your stress response.** A rollicking laugh fires up and then cools down your stress response, and it can increase and then decrease your heart rate and blood pressure. The result? A good, relaxed feeling.

- **Soothe tension.** Laughter can also stimulate circulation and aid muscle relaxation; this helps reduce some of the physical symptoms of stress.

Long-Term Effects

Laughter isn't just a quick pick-me-up, though. It's also good for you over the long term. Laughter may:

- **Improve your immune system.** Negative thoughts manifest into chemical reactions that can affect your body by bringing more stress into your system and decreasing your immunity. In contrast, positive thoughts can release neuropeptides that help fight stress and potentially more serious illnesses.

- **Relieve pain.** Laughter may ease pain by causing the body to produce its own natural painkillers.

- **Increase personal satisfaction.** Laughter can also make it easier to cope with difficult situations. It also helps you connect with other people.

- **Improve your mood.** Many people experience depression, sometimes due to chronic illnesses. Laughter can help lessen your depression and anxiety and may make you feel happier.

A good sense of humor helps us laugh, but it's not necessary. My grandma Irène was a bit naive and a tad too literal. She rarely got a joke, but she still laughed at things she found amusing, including herself. And even when she didn't get the joke, she laughed anyway. She liked laughing with others. My kids in their teenage years would mock me, "Mom, we're laughing *at* you, not with you."

"So what?" I'd retort. "As long as we're all laughing, we'll have a good time."

I get messy. I can be a klutz. If I trip and have a nice fall (but don't get hurt), I can laugh about it, giving others the freedom to laugh at how ridiculous I looked without adding insult to injury. If I do get hurt, laughing will momentarily distract me from the pain.

Once at church, while helping my grandson with toilet training, he failed to hold his artillery down, and I got blasted with a healthy stream of pee. People outside the restroom had to wonder, "What's going on in there?" as I burst out in hilarity. Then I reminded him, "Next time, hold your penis down, please." It was funny, and God made it happen in a room with running water. It all came out in the wash.

Let's face it, sometimes we do funny things unintentionally. We find ourselves in humiliating but amusing circumstances. One secret to staying young at heart—laugh at yourself. Others are going to. Don't let them have all the fun. Do you want to live well? Laugh!

Always Looking Good

Doris's sporty sense of humor keeps her cruising through life. Like a '56 T-Bird with porthole windows, Doris Lowe is a classic. She's never quit looking good, and her style is being in style. When scarves came back into fashion, Doris donned old and new ones tied in the most current fashion. As a professional seamstress, she tracked the trends. Doris never dresses in an outdated manner. Oh, she may wear vintage clothing but always with a *contemporary* twist. Her daughters and granddaughters don't hesitate to gift her with new accessories because they know she'll put them to good use. They're happy to give Doris fashion advice because she's glad to take it.

Her silver hair reveals her contentment with her age. Doris keeps it cut short, but not too short, and stylish, not trendy. She paints her face with a natural look: a light moisturizing foundation, a bit of cheek color, and a light swoosh of mascara. Enhancing her face's pleasant, timeless glow doesn't take much.

Pressed and put together, Doris shows the world she knows what's happening. She cares for those around her by caring about her appearance. People are not put off by her looks. Like the virtuous woman of Proverbs 31 dressed in purple, Doris's visage radiates nobility. She's a princess, a daughter of the King of Kings. And her excellent grooming reveals this reality.

Choose to Look Good

My first career revolved around looking good. As a licensed cosmetologist, I was committed to making my clients look their best. And keeping up my appearance served as good advertising. I haven't worked in a salon since I was twenty-three, but I still watch style trends. Working part-time retail helps. In my professional opinion, nothing betrays a woman's age more than a *stagnant* sense of style. If your clothing, makeup, or hair scream the year you graduated from high school or college, you're telling the world, "I'm out of touch." Is that what a grand soul wants to communicate? No! So please, accept a few professional pointers.

Clothing — I realize we all have different budgets, and not everyone gets a discount from working retail. Doris's modest fixed income didn't keep her from nice clothing. Hang on to pieces you love, the ones you look and feel great in. Even if those pieces aren't trendy now, they will come back in style—and vintage is way cooler than retro! When you buy something new, make sure you already have a few coordinating pieces in your closet. Classic clothing can easily be updated with costume jewelry. And some new pieces of clothing can get extra *wow* from old jewelry. Shop with young women. Be *open* to their advice. Ask that cute twenty-something sales associate what she thinks when you're trying things on in the fitting room. Window shopping will keep you current and in the know. Pay attention not only to clothes but also to hair and make-up; these trends change too.

A woman I know graduated from high school in the mid-1950s. Her penciled-in eyebrows betrayed her. She last tweaked her hairdo in the early eighties, when white women sported afros. When I first met her, sculpted brows had not come back. Now bold, defined brows are all the rage. However, it wouldn't hurt for her to update her hairstyle and let the 'fro go.

Hair — Your natural color will never clash with your skin. Isn't God amazing?! And at the writing of this book, platinum is the new gold standard—twenty-somethings flock to salons to bleach away their youthful color and get grey. However, if you just can't handle God's highlights, you should know that as your hair loses pigment, so does your skin.

To maintain a natural appearance, you should never color your hair more than a shade or two darker than its present natural color. Nothing screams, "Fake!" like jet-black hair on a woman in her eighties. It looked good on her when she was twenty. Now the stark contrast makes her look old and *uncomfortable* with her age. Some of the best-looking blondes I know were dark brunettes in their twenties.

Currently, crazy unnatural hair color is in. Do you like hot pink locks? Go for it! Do you prefer pretty pastels? Now's the time to do it. I'm all for fun, fake hair color as long as it's fashionable. These colors aren't trying to hide anything. They shout, "I'm bold! I'm fun!" But when they shout, "I'm out," let them grow away!

My close friend Nancy decided to let her natural platinum grow in. Then, she over-brightened it with color shampoo. Her hair took on a pale lavender glow. In the past, she would have been pegged as a blue-haired old lady. Today her faux pas looks quite chic. The shade looks lovely on her, which is my only guideline for artificial color—pick a color that looks good on you.

Finally, length no longer matters. We baby boomers abolished the old rule of no long hair after forty. Whatever you choose to do—clean, well-trimmed, and stylish—always looks nice.

Makeup — First of all, it's not necessary. A bare face is never offensive. Going without makeup reveals satisfaction with how God made you. Moisturizer, however, is essential, and not just on our faces. As we age, our natural production of oil decreases. Replacing moisture helps reduce micro-cracks in our skin. Your skin is your largest organ and your first line of defense against germs. Take good care of it. Exfoliate and moisturize regularly. Plus, a dewy glow just looks better than chalky dryness. Here are some pointers to keep in mind for those who like applying makeup.

As the years pile on, less is more. I recently met a woman about ten years my senior. I found myself distracted by all the foundation that had settled into her wrinkles. I thought, "She's one of those ladies who tries on clothing and leaves her face behind." You've seen it. You pick up a garment in the store to try on, and all over the neckline is an unconscientious woman's make-up. Eeew! *Not cool.*

Regardless of what your Mary Kay consultant or the woman at the Lancôme counter tells you, a full face of foundation is not the best way to even out your skin tone. They make a living selling cosmetics. I recommend using concealer on your dark spots and blending it well. Doing so leaves your natural skin tone exposed and saves you from choosing the wrong color foundation. If your career requires public speaking, wearing foundation on top of the concealer works, but for everyday wear, let your skin breathe.

Those who like a simple, natural look are safe. These women play it safe with a light application of softer colors. Like our bare-faced friends, they won't distract anyone. What's trickier is a good application of a full face of makeup.

Like clothes and hair, make-up trends come and go. Twiggy's paper-thin brows of the 1960s got booted off stage by Brook Shields's bushy brows of the 1980s. Thick brows, thin brows, natural brows, lined brows—these looks rotate in and out. Lip colors go from glossy to matte, and bright to neutral. Eye shadow does the same. If you enjoy wearing it all, foundation, eyeshadow, liner, lipstick, etc., please, *be aware* of current trends. Sit with a young esthetician, and let her show you how to apply today's latest look. Do that at least every five years, or go with a more natural look.

I recently met a missionary. She didn't have to tell me she graduated from college in the eighties because her lipliner said it all. Not only was the look outdated, but it wasn't applied well. This woman, lovely on the inside with a deep commitment to serving others, muffles her message with distracting lipstick.

No doubt my distraction with superficial beauty comes off as shallow and petty, but God wired me as a visual person. Please, understand I enjoyed my conversations with these sisters in Christ. Yet their appearances distracted me. God created me with an eye for color and design. I appreciate the beauty of His creation. I know He's designed others in the same way, but not everyone sees the way an artist does. As ambassadors for Christ, let's cultivate an awareness that there are visually wired people who consider poor appearances as a put-off. We don't want our *packaging* to mute our *message*. Lovely inside *and out*—that's grand.

Never a Gold Ring in a Pig's Snout

A woman who laughs well and looks great can still be a pig. "Like a gold ring in a pig's snout is a beautiful woman without discretion" (Proverbs 11:22). Being classy requires discretion, another of Doris' admirable attributes—a quality I depended on that desperate day I picked up the phone.

"Hi, Doris. It's Teri. Do you have any time to get together this week? I'm in a terrible conflict with a good friend and need some advice."

Doris carved out some space to meet with me. She invited me to her place. At that time, my home was still bustling with children and teenagers. They needn't hear about my dilemma or interrupt my conversation with Doris. Meeting in her home provided us with privacy and quiet. I was in a difficult situation. I needed wisdom *and* discretion.

As a pastor's wife, I can't always afford to share as openly with other women as I'd like. My circle of trusted confidants is small. I knew I could count on Doris not only for counsel, but also discretion and empathy. She was a pastor's wife, too.

Doris spent most of her adult life as a pastor's wife. When Loyd retired early in his fifties because of heart disease, he and Doris continued actively serving in the church. Loyd took the office of deacon and brought Community Baptist Church through some tough times. Doris taught children's church and Sunday School and mentored younger women. In the pastoral search that led CBC to call my husband as their senior pastor, Bill and I speculated on which of the deacons interviewing him would be the most challenging (once the honeymoon is over, at least one church leader contends for power). We thought it would be Loyd. How wrong we were.

Loyd and Doris humbled themselves under Bill's leadership and rose to be our greatest advocates. It became evident after serving with them for a year that their calling into pastoral ministry was not just for a time but a lifetime. Loyd pastored. So, twenty years after leaving vocational ministry, the church called Loyd as Pastor Emeritus. Loyd and Doris regained the title of the work they'd been doing all along.

Doris seemed just as thrilled as Loyd with this new season. It validated their call and reinforced their position of influence among their fellow worshippers. It also meant I now had a pastor who wasn't my husband and a *pastor's wife* to be my confidant. After a decade of ministry, this was the first church situation to afford me this luxury. Doris and Loyd prayed for and with us through the next nine years of ministry. They were privy to things that those outside of pastoral leadership are often unaware of, like how a pastor's wife has a horrible falling out with a close, long-time friend.

Doris met with me on several occasions to help me work through the fight I had with my old friend. She listened to me read the letters my friend and I wrote to each other (this friend lived out of town) and helped me revise what I wrote. She handed me Kleenex when I cried and cried with me. When I was wrong, Doris told me so. She asked hard questions that helped me see things from my friend's point of view. She wanted to get the whole story before giving any advice.

Doris helped me do all I could to save that friendship. In the end, she helped me let it go when my friend chose not to reconcile. And all the while, she kept it to herself.

Choose to be Discrete

I mentioned in earlier chapters the value of being a good listener, but there's more to discretion than keeping your mouth shut. A discreet woman listens with two ears. She hears both sides of the story. Proverbs 18:13 tells us, "If one gives an answer before he hears, it is his folly and shame." When a friend comes to us with a problem, do we quickly take their side, or do we help them consider the other person involved? Discretion takes an objective look at the whole situation *before* giving counsel. There is always more than one side to a problem. A discreet woman understands that and seeks to gain insight on the matter before giving advice.

Doris never said, "I know how you feel." This show of empathy works in small matters, but that phrase sounds trite in someone suffering real difficulty. We hear it and think, "No, you *don't* know how I feel!"

The son of a close friend recently committed suicide. He was twenty-seven; I'd known him since he was a little boy. He was a deep thinker and an excellent writer. This quote from a piece he wrote haunts me. "I could walk miles in your shoes, but I cannot feel the blisters on your feet." We cannot know someone else's hurt. Genuine empathy requires understanding and identifying with their emotion without the pretense of omniscience. Discretion keeps her pain in the backseat while another's hurt drives.

Emotional reactions vary from person to person. We cannot know how intensely another person feels in any situation. I've lost three children. I murdered the first—I had an abortion at seventeen before I became a Christian. The second was stillborn at twenty-six weeks gestation. I miscarried the third. These losses don't mean I know how another woman feels about her loss of a child. Even if I never lost a child, I know loss hurts. That's the wisdom of "Weep with those who weep" (Romans 12:15). Weeping turns sympathy into empathy. We go from simply identifying to internalizing and sharing someone's pain. Doris mastered this skill. She only spoke when she knew what to say. If she didn't, her silence spoke wisdom. The best thing to say when you don't know what to say is nothing, followed by, "I am so sorry." I need to learn this skill.

My compulsion to play Holy Spirit has gotten me into trouble several times. Needed truth spoken in love is not always a welcome gift. There is a time to share hard words—but only after much prayer. Let's be certain God wants us to be His messenger. God doesn't *need us* to communicate His truth, but He may *choose* to use us that way. Stephen Covey's advice, "Seek first to understand, then to be understood," provides valuable insight into real understanding. Understanding puts the needs of others before our own. It recognizes we do not know another's thoughts, motives, or circumstances. It has the humility to listen, question, and allow our paradigm to shift when needed. Understanding flows from an open heart with an open mind and applies wisdom gleaned from God's Word. Discretion embraces understanding. Oh, Lord, teach us discretion!

Doris received the best compliment I have ever heard. Her daughter, Debbie, said of her, "She was always a lady." Doris's other daughter, Laura, agreed. Those women never witnessed their mom being anything but discrete. They grew up enjoying Doris's fun-loving sense of humor. They benefitted from learning Doris's good grooming skills and eye for style. And they flourished under the wings of a discreet mama who protected everyone's dignity. Doris was always a lady—a classy lady. And this elegant woman enjoyed singing new songs.

Enjoying God's New Mercies

Doris's daughters transformed the modest sanctuary of Community Baptist Church into a lovely party venue. Lace tablecloths covered each table. Golden ribbons around vases of white flowers adorned the round tables. A trellis draped with tulle took center stage on the platform. Doris and Loyd's clan of children, grandchildren, siblings, nieces, and nephews gathered there along with friends and their church family. We all came to celebrate their fiftieth wedding anniversary.

Together, we shared stories, laughed, and ate scrumptious food. Loyd and Doris honored the Lord who made them one flesh; they credited the One who empowered them to keep their vows with His love. Their daughters shared testimonies of the loving family Loyd and Doris created. We lifted prayers of thanksgiving. And we *sang.*

We sang some of the Lowe's favorite hymns and heard their grandsons sing some new songs. These boys played various instruments, including drums. Doris and Loyd beamed with joy. Hearing the new generation—their offspring—praise God with new songs confirmed they successfully passed the baton of faith. They understood the reality that new mercies require new music. And they were always willing to learn new lyrics and melodies. Are we?

Choose to Sing New Songs

Using my Strong's Concordance, I discovered that encouragement to "sing a new song" is given nine times. Yet, the Bible never instructs us to sing old songs. The closest direction I could find on doing something old came from the prophet Jeremiah:

> "Thus says the Lord: 'Stand by the roads, and look, and ask for the ancient paths, where the good way is; and walk in it, and find rest for your souls.' But they said, 'We will not walk in it.'" (Jeremiah 6:16)

That "ancient path" refers to walking with God as Adam and Eve did in the Garden of Eden. Adam and his wife enjoyed intimacy with their Creator. They knew God. Do we? God's mercies are new every morning (Lamentations 3:22–23). His new mercies call for new songs of praise. God teaches us that even in heaven, His people will sing *new* songs (Revelation 5:9 and 14:3). He declares, "I am making *all* things new" (Revelation 21:5). I discovered *more* on my brief concordance search.

I learned that the word "old" in the Bible most often refers to age. A funny fact about old believers: we tend to enjoy the music we learned when we were first born again. That makes sense. Like children enjoy the lullabies of their infancy, we feel secure with familiar music—and there's nothing wrong with that. But I don't want to be old. I want to grow grand. I desire to *continue* to see God at work in the world. I want to sing about what He's doing *today*. Isn't our infinite God worthy of an unending variety of praise music? New generations create new music; I look forward to singing the music they enjoy with my grandkids, unlike the woman who complained to me in church.

"I *really* don't like those drums. And I wish we would do more hymns." This well-meaning woman in her late seventies confided to me, her pastor's wife.

I put my arm around her shoulder and, as gently as I could muster, replied, "Gertrude (not her name), aren't you glad both of your grandsons join you each week for worship?"

"Yes."

"And they're both quite musical, aren't they?"

"Yes."

"Do you think they like the newer songs we sing?"

"Yes."

"And we do still sing hymns, right?"

"Yes, we do. But not as many as I'd like."

"Well, Gertrude, I'm going to pray that you'll learn to appreciate singing new songs with your grandsons each week. Remember, the Bible does call us to sing new songs."

Like Doris's new accessories spruced up an old outfit, new songs adorn aged saints and make them *grand*.

Remember I compared Doris to a classic T-Bird? A car is only useful if it runs, and the best classics do. Like well-restored engines hum with new power, well-refreshed souls hum new songs. Grand souls cruise through life, singing modern music about the fresh ways they see God working. Doris's example taught me living classy happens when I choose to laugh (appropriately, of course), look good, exercise discretion, and sing new songs.

Glancing up in my closet, I see the couple of hats I own. A fabulous photo of Doris flashes in my head. In the picture, taken at a wedding, she wears a winter-white chapeau with a narrow brim, satin ribbon, and a finely netted blusher. She looks more elegant than Queen Elizabeth. If we're daughters of the King of Kings, isn't it fitting that we display the class of nobility? Let's plan to be stylish and discreet. Let's keep laughing and singing new tunes through all the years God appoints us. Like my dear friend Doris, let's choose to be class acts.

Choice Meditations

1. Read Proverbs 15:15. What two perspectives are revealed in this verse? What light does this shed on our power to choose?

2. Read Proverbs 31:10–31. How does this virtuous woman care for others? How does she care for her soul? How does she care for her outer appearance? What does she spend most of her time doing? How about the least amount of her time? How do her priorities reveal an appropriate amount of time on physical appearance?

3. Read Proverbs 11:22. How does a lack of discretion affect a woman's appearance?

4. According to Psalm 33:1–3, is singing a new song optional? Describe the music of this new song. What is God's opinion of this music?

Choice Considerations

1. Have you laughed today? How about yesterday? Do you remember the last good laugh you had? Write about it.

2. How will you choose to have a merry heart today?

3. Before you leave your house, how do you beautify your inner self? What do you do to improve your outer appearance? Which do you spend the most time on? Which do you find more enjoyable?

4. When was the last time someone in their twenties complimented your appearance in some way? What did they compliment?

5. In light of our fuller understanding, how are you displaying discretion? In what ways could you be more discreet?

Choice Actions

1. For the next week, choose to find something amusing each day.

2. Recount a funny thing that happened to you and laugh with your audience of co-workers, friends, or family members.

3.

Become a student of God's sense of humor as you read Scripture.

4. Clean out your closet and make-up drawer, so you know what you have. And discover what you need. Then call your favorite twenty-something friend (yes, daughters count) and go shopping with a list in hand.

5. Review my professional advice in this chapter and take a long, hard look in the mirror. Pick one thing you can do better and do it.

6. Do a word study on discretion in the Bible.

7. Permit your friends to tell you when you're being indiscreet.

8. Go to YouTube. Find a new-to-you song, one you have never heard, and learn it. Sing it!

9. During church worship, when you don't like a particular song, choose to focus on the lyrics and lift them to the Lord as a sacrifice of praise.

10. Ask a young person, maybe even a child, which song they enjoyed most. Then thank God for the joy that little one could have.

13

Quiet Kay

Living in the Hush of Holiness

Set your mind on things above, not on things on the earth. For you died, and your life is hidden with Christ in God. When Christ, who is our life, appears, then you also will appear with Him in glory.
Colossians 3:2–4

The pleasant aromas of bread baking and coffee brewing wafted through the crowded fellowship hall. I stood with a cup of tea in one hand and a homemade roll in the other. Who should I talk to, I wondered. A short, white-haired woman approached me. A smile lit her face, and the love of Jesus glowed in her pale aqua eyes.

"Hello, Teri. Welcome to Grace!" Kay chirped.

Grace Baptist Church of Manhattan, Kansas called my husband, Bill, as their interim pastor. Finally, after a two-year search, we had a new church family. Eventually, the church would call him permanently, but at this point, we didn't know how long we'd stay. After wandering in a three-year wilderness, my heart churned with expectations of finally settling into a new ministry. Yet, I also had concerns about how things would go in this church. Division threatened this assembly's unity. I resolved to love this church for as long as God left us here. Kay is one of those people that makes loving Grace Baptist Church easy. She continued, "I'm Kay Bascom, Dr. Charles's wife."

"Oh," I replied with a grateful smile, "you're the dear folks who've looked out for Jon the last couple of weeks. Thanks so much for opening your home to our son."

This move had come as Jon's senior year of high school began. He'd had a great attitude about the whole ordeal. He and Bill had moved out the month before while I stayed in Oregon to pack up and sell the house there. Since school had started, and Jon didn't have a car while Bill was helping me move, Jon stayed with the Bascom's and went to school with their grandson, Alex, also a recent transplant to Kansas. He was a missionary kid from Kenya.

"Your son's been a pleasure to have," Kay assured me. "He and Alex really seem to have hit it off. They've been enjoying football practice. Here are some pictures I took. I thought you'd enjoy some copies." She reached into her purse, pulled out an envelope, and handed it to me.

How can you not love a woman who thinks to give you pictures of your kid?

An Eternal Soul Fights Finitude

Since that day, Kay has handed me several envelopes filled with photos; a Bible study group, a women's retreat, a mission's brunch—all recorded on film. If she attends an event, you'll likely see her camera flash just as she flashes you a smile. Every church family needs a shutterbug; Kay Bascom is ours. One day I asked about all the pictures she took, "So Kay, I was wondering what you do with all your pictures?"

"I put them in albums. I have yet to do what my mother-in-law advised. She told me to write names and dates on the back. Instead, I put comment notes beside them in the album. Photos are my fight against finitude. And my battle to keep fellowship with those far away," Kay declares. She continues, "I always make double prints so I can send them to the friends I was with at the time. I just sent out several this past week." But her desire to capture memories goes well beyond the pages of her albums.

The first time Kay invited Bill and me for a meal, Dr. and Mrs. Bascom told us about constructing their two-bedroom log cabin.

"It was a community effort," Dr. Bascom assured us. He then proceeded to share the highlights of the construction. As Charles finished his rousing retelling, Kay chimed in.

"See the plank up there," she said, pointing to the large board hanging from the beam over the dividing wall between the living room and the dining area where we were seated. Signatures covered the face of the plank. "We asked everyone who helped to sign their name. We are grateful for each of them and want to remember them all."

Kay also writes. She's a published author of several Bible studies and a mission book concerning the Marxist revolution in Ethiopia, *Hidden Triumph in Ethiopia.* That book was one story of several dozen that Kay wrote based on interviews with believers and the persecution they suffered under the Marxist regime. Kay took pictures of every person she interviewed so she could look them in the eyes and remember their voices as she wrote their accounts. A 350-page book entitled *Ethiopia Ablaze* resulted from those interviews and revealed the history of these persecuted saints. The publisher wanted one tidy story that represented the collection. Kay chose to tell Negussie Kumbi's story; the rest got shelved. That was twenty years ago.

A missionary from Germany recently came across some of Kay's research on the internet. He contacted Kay and walked her through publishing her entire manuscript to benefit ministers bound for Ethiopia and to encourage the Ethiopian believers as they again encounter tribulation. This book, *Overcomers* (published by Wipf & Stock), is currently available. All those pictures Kay took to help her write now appear in print alongside the individuals' stories. God chose to use Kay's seemingly forgotten hours of labor. Kay's rediscovered manuscript reminds me of a truth I learned long ago: God doesn't waste *anything*. When we walk with Him, all the trials we traverse, the effort we invest, *even* in mundane tasks, He uses to build His Kingdom and edify His people.

Only God knows how many of us have benefited from Kay's recording endeavors. Currently, Kay is working on a project she calls "Life with Charlie." In it, she shares various accounts of her sixty-one years of marriage. She has no intention of having it published. She writes it to herself. It is a labor of love, a way to cope with widowhood and leave a legacy for their grandchildren. Yet, when she and I and the other three writers of the Wellspring Writers Group gather, we plead like excited schoolchildren, "Kay, please read to us some more Charlie stories!" Anne Lamont includes a chapter in her book, *Bird by Bird*, entitled Writing a Present. Anne makes the case that writing just to gift a person you love is a great reason to write. Kay writes presents. Will we bless our families with our words, memories, and experiences?

❧

Choose to Preserve Your History

Our memories resemble scrapbooks more than timelines. Snapshots of moments, some eventful, others ordinary, clutter the pages of our minds in random arrangements. We often find it hard to remember the actual order of events. So, we snap pictures and write journal entries.

Like Kay, I'm a shutterbug. True confession, when my children were little, my camera belonged on the kitchen counter. No, it was not cluttering my counter; it was *accessible.* And I used it regularly. When my toddler and the other one-year-old I babysat covered my kitchen floor and themselves in corn starch, I clicked the shutter instead of shuddering. When my eight-year-old bit the dust on our crowded swing set, my camera's flash caught her bruise on film after I gave her ice for her shiner. Fuji made millions on my investment in film, but the pictures our family enjoys today are worth more to us than all the profits of Fuji and Kodak combined.

Back in the days before Skype and Facetime, like Kay, I always made double prints. I sent the doubles to my parents, who lived 2000 miles away. That's how they watched their grandchildren grow up. Later, when I decided to make a scrapbook for each of my four children, my mom gave me her set of copies of all the photos. She had sorted them into four albums, one for each child. My mom's organizing efforts made the job of scrapbooking easy. My children and I benefitted from my mother's labor to preserve a heritage for her grandchildren. Today each of my children has three volumes of handmade albums with journal entries about places, people, and events.

During a visit with my oldest daughter's family, I mentioned to my Star Wars-obsessed grandchildren that their mother once dressed up as Queen Amidala. I went to the trunk, pulled out the scrapbook, and showed them their mom as a kid, face white, lips painted small and red like a geisha, and those famous Amidala red-dotted cheeks. The kids smiled and kept thumbing through the pages, enjoying the discovery that their mama was a kid once too. Those scrapbooks, filled with pictures and words, express my love for my family and transmit a legacy of love for future generations. Like Kay, I too, fight finitude. History may be passed, but it need not be forgotten. After all, it brought us to our current location. And our past remains part of the driving force that takes us into our futures. Kay's history certainly affected her future.

For Kay so Loved the World

The day Kay said "I do" to the future Doctor Bascom, she had no idea where God would take them. This young Kansas girl shared a home state with *The Wizard of Oz's* Dorothy, but her perspective on a home was vastly different. Kay chose to follow Jesus in her college years. She made her home in Christ. However, Kay's introduction to Ethiopia happened in her childhood. She told us about it in our writer's group one day.

> "My folks used to tell a story, mimicking a quote when I was six, lisping it with my baby teeth out. We had gone for a picnic on dusty back roads in Doniphan County and had come home coated coffee-colored brown. I was heard to say, "We're all becoming E-ti-o-pians!" Why would a Kansas child respond that way? My guess is that I'd been hearing my parents talking about the news of Mussolini's invasion of Ethiopia in 1937 and seeing pictures in the newspaper.

> In later life, to my surprise, the Lord sent us to Africa and bonded us deeply with Ethiopia. The Acts chapter eight account of the Ethiopian eunuch's conversion became one of my favorite stories. Its outworking

stretched from the first century to my own life. I can't help celebrating the Holy Spirit's choice of Ethiopia to represent what our Lord Jesus called 'to the ends of the earth.' To my earth, too!"

"Many people go abroad to travel; most go to see the world and observe new cultures. I found that going as a missionary to our assignment gave us a calling and an equipping that were spiritual gifts. The Spirit provides a depth of identification with the new culture's people, an identification founded in love—not ours, but His planted in our hearts. That love is not just general but specific. You come to love particular people He puts in your path. For us, it was people like Blind Endalla and Sahle Tilahun in Language School, Wandaro, Marta, Nega in Soddu, Negussie, Yeshiwas, and Merissa at a later time, and the list goes on." (These people turn up in the book *Overcomers*.)

It took only six weeks to raise support for the Bascom's first trip. Charles and Kay spent ten years serving and caring for the physical and spiritual needs of the people of Ethiopia and Sudan. She describes their mission service as "long-term short-termers" as they traveled back and forth through the years.

Now, back in the United States for good, Kay still loves the world. She regularly engages the many international students and their families attending Kansas State University. She fellowships regularly with people who come to our church from all over the globe.

Currently, Kay helped an Ethiopian family of five negotiate their new life in America. They immigrated with a Diversity Visa; basically, they won the immigration lottery. The US government issued them green cards, but they came with only what they could carry on the plane. They had to find housing, jobs, everything. These folks are Christians and started coming to Grace Baptist when they arrived. What a blessing Kay has been to them. She's familiar with the foods they enjoy and understands their culture. She understands their broken English and helps them navigate finding better employment (both the mom and dad worked at McDonald's). The dad has a master's degree. Can you imagine coming to a country and losing your career? It's tough for this family, but Kay's love provides a cushion for them. However, her passion for God's creation doesn't end with people. She also delights in trees.

Kay and Charles often wandered through the trees in the park of Keats, Kansas. She even mapped them, listing the variety of each tree. Oaks, Maples, and Elms each have a place on her map and in her heart. Kansas provides a challenging climate for tree growing. Trees here grow by nurture, not nature. Kay wanted to nurture a few more in the park. She also wanted to foster a well-educated community.

> I thought her involvement with the Parks and Recreation department of Keats, Kansas, was intentional, but when I asked, Kay told me: "The Lord pushed me out into the community. I had no idea how much I would need to do to give my map away. I was told I couldn't. That led to having to go to the Park Department, the Lions Club, which oversees the park, and the county commissioners to start a process of asking for a grant from the Caroline Pine Foundation—which would cover half the cost of completing the plantings proposed in the original park plan. The community had to cover the other half mostly by donating funds for memorial trees. Securing the grant led to eighty new trees being planted, with memorial tree markers and variety-explaining stakes. My little map was never used because the Park

Deptment created a very complete technical one with all the new plantings labeled correctly."

This community involvement gives Kay's faith a platform to reveal her love for the Creator and His creation.

Many people in their eighties feel isolated. Not Kay. This year alone, she's hosted so many overnight guests that she couldn't tell me how many when I asked her. She teaches Bible studies and provides great insight to her fellow Wellspring Writers. She chooses not only to withdraw at times to write but, most importantly, to re-engage with the world she loves.

Choose to be Involved in the World

Some of the most vital work offers no pay. Who pays the mamas doing the night shift with a colicky baby or the wives who care for disabled husbands? Who tutors underprivileged children falling through the cracks in public school or helps illiterate adults learn to read? Who hands out food at food pantries or cooks meals at missions for the homeless? Volunteers do!

Retirement from a full-time job or being a well-kept woman allows some of us the freedom to work without pay. If we don't volunteer in our churches and communities, essential things will be left undone. Choosing to be involved in the world, to do hard work with no financial compensation, makes a woman genuinely grand. It frees her from isolation—a solution for loneliness. And the community benefits.

My mom chose involvement at the local elementary school. She volunteered to tutor children who needed extra help learning to read. There are library and prison programs to teach illiterate adults to read. There are homeless shelters and soup kitchens that need more hands. There are neighborhood watch programs that need eyes and ears. If your neighborhood doesn't have one, you could start it. What a great way to get to know your neighbors. The older we get, the more we *need* those neighbors. No matter your age, there is always something you can do. I just heard on the local news of a ninety-seven-year-old gentleman who repairs books at the public library.

Grace Baptist Church is the largest congregation my husband has pastored. With so many women to befriend at church, it would be easy to neglect developing relationships outside my holy huddle. But God calls me *out*. "Go, and make disciples," Jesus commanded. So, I chose to go back to working retail part-time. I decided to walk across the road and meet my neighbor. These choices give me opportunities to be involved in the lives of unchurched people.

God had to give Kay a nudge into community involvement. What might God be nudging you to do? As long as God gives you breath, He'll give you work to do. In whatever way we choose, let's choose to stay involved.

Death Breaks in Like a Thief

Two years had passed since Jon and Alex first met. Both boys longed for their homelands. Two years ahead of Alex in school, Jon graduated and moved back to Oregon. Alex's home was Kenya. Finding relief from homesickness eluded him. That September, I traveled to Oregon to visit Jon. One morning, at about 8 a.m., my phone rang.

"Teri, this is Nancy." Nancy Swihart was a close friend of the Bascoms. "I felt you and Jon should hear this firsthand before things come up on social media. Alex is dead. It appears he committed suicide. I'm so sorry. I know this is going to be tough for Jon."

We wept. I thanked Nancy for her thoughtfulness. I prayed for each member of the Bascom family, including Kay. Then I woke my son to tell him his best friend in Kansas had killed himself. That day Jon and I packed up early to drive back to Kansas for the funeral. It was the longest, most painful road trip we'd ever taken. We talked, sharing memories of Alex. We cried. We sat dumbfounded—numbed by confusion and loss. Silence filled many of those miles.

I thought back to Marcia, Alex's mom, greeting me at Riley County High School the day the boys went in to register—joy and hope were shining in her smile. I wept for the weight of her empty arms and shattered dreams. I felt survivor's guilt as I sat next to my son, knowing her son lay beyond her reach. I thought of Kay and Charles, losing a grandchild on the verge of manhood. I can't even imagine their pain! Death's tragic intrusion robbed them of their grandson.

Jon and I attended Alex's visitation the night before the funeral. As Jon lingered at the casket, I waited in the back. Kay approached me and quietly inquired, "How is Jon doing?" Her concern for my son came before any expression of her pain. I don't remember the rest of our conversation. I do remember her composure and her compassion for others grieving over Alex.

A year later, I witnessed the same remarkable composure as she and her three sons each shared their memories of Charles at his funeral. Yes, Kay lost her husband a year after losing Alex. She embraced grief as her unwelcome companion by allowing herself to cry, reflect, and withdraw as needed. Yet Kay refused to be mastered by grief. She refrained from self-pity, isolation, and retaliation against the hand of the Sovereign.

Kay blessed God, never doubting His goodness, continually thankful for what He gave instead of lamenting what He had taken. Kay's attitude was never "Why me?" or "God, how could

You?" but rather, "Why not me?" and "How can I honor You, Lord, through this pain?" She showed me—and our whole church family—what it looks like to grieve with hope.

Choose to Grieve with Hope

Embracing grief is the job of the living. Only living souls grieve. Only those who walk through it continue living. Grand souls endure the extreme highs and lows that crash against their hearts in unexpected waves. Yet, like rocks in the ocean, they remain firmly planted in the land of the living. Those who choose to be buried by grief die while they still have breath—like my Grandma Erma did when her son (my father) died.

How do I grieve with hope? This question plagued my mind when my dad passed away. I love to hear the testimonies of those who diligently pray for years for their unsaved parents. Then their parents finally come to Christ. I praise God with them for His mercy and kindness. That is not my story. My dad, a professing deist (there is a God who created the world but does not control it), expressed hostility concerning Jesus as the Savior. He called Jesus "a liar—the greatest con man who ever lived!" According to my belief system (Biblical Christianity), those without Christ go to Hell. Never hearing him repent. Watching him perish. These kicked me in the gut like a raging stallion. What about mercy? What hope could I have for my father?

God—my Abba—in compassion, came to me in my pain. His Holy Spirit whispered truth through Scripture and an old hymn. It began with the melody. The afternoon before he died, my oldest daughter and I visited with him; he was incoherent, so we just hummed and sang old hymns. We later found out that *In the Garden*—the last song we sang to him—my dad had heard at his father's funeral. Might this reminder have prompted my father to turn to Jesus? The Lord reminded me, "Shall not the Judge of the whole earth do right?" (Genesis 25:18). I opened my Bible and read the story. I found myself with Abraham—after he had fervently interceded for Lot (like I had for my father)—looking into a valley. Abraham gazed out at the cities of the plain: Sodom and Gomorrah; I looked into the Valley of the Shadow of Death. Abraham watched the destruction of Sodom. There is no Biblical evidence he ever saw Lot again. Yet, Abraham rested in understanding that the Judge of all the earth *does* right.

My hope in God's mercy will not be fully realized until I, too, pass through the veil. I will either find my dad made a deathbed plea for forgiveness, or I will feel the gentle fingers of Jesus wiping my tears away. Let's remember God is love, and He is merciful—or no one would be saved. No one deserves heaven. My hope rests in His righteousness alone. I believe—no matter how wrong it seems from my perspective—the Judge of all the earth will do right. Do you?

Should God give us long lives, death will rob us of many loved ones. Yet the Apostle Paul gives us this encouragement, "But we do not want you to be uninformed, brothers, about those who are asleep (those who have died), that you may not grieve as others do who have no hope" (1 Thessalonians 4:13). As Kay and I discovered, grieving with hope requires us to humble our hearts under the mighty hand of our Maker.

❦

Looking at the World Through God-Colored Glasses

Despite Kay's assurance that her dear Charlie is with Jesus, she experiences loneliness. Loneliness often plagues the bereaved.

"Without Charlie, how could I not be lonely? Everywhere I look, there are reminders of his absence. Every chair. Every book. It's like the balloon of your life has lost all its air and falls to the ground, limp. Now it's up to the Holy Spirit to inflate you and carry you along." Kay is learning to let the Lord be her husband.

Kay enjoyed many good things in her life but also endured great hardships. Her father died in a plane crash the week she graduated from high school. Kay's mother almost died of a heart attack days before she and Charlie married. She survived a narrow escape from Ethiopia when the Marxists overthrew the government in the mid-seventies. Through it all, God developed patience in her—a quiet confidence that waits on the Lord.

Kay's quiet spirit comes from her confidence in God. She lives her life based—not on how she *feels*—but on *Who God is* and His purposes for her. She submits to His sanctifying work and seeks to be cleansed by His Word, sanctified by His truth. She longs to be holy because her God is holy. And through this process, Kay's developed her Father's eyes and the wisdom gained from viewing the world from His perspective.

Several sweet, well-aged women attend Grace Baptist, but only Kay Bascom earned the reputation of resident Bible scholar. When she teaches Bible study, women who don't usually participate in regular studies come out just to learn from Kay. A young man giving announcements one Sunday morning said, "Kay Bascom will be leading this Bible Study. Men, make sure you encourage your wives to go. I know if Kay's teaching, it will be great!"

After all the words she's typed, Kay reminds us regularly at Wellspring Writers, "It's not about being published or making money. Writing is simply obeying God's call." Kay lives what she teaches, and by her example, we learn the value of humility.

One day at Wellspring Writers, I vented my discouragement and frustration. I was finding it difficult to navigate my transition from homemaking to writing. Housekeeping imposed upon my writing time. And frankly, I was tired of housekeeping.

"Teri, remember you still have a husband and home to care for." Kay gently reminded me. As a recent empty-nester, I needed reminding that my identity is in Christ, not the work He gives me. The work He's given me matters, but I needed to embrace His priorities in my life.

Once upon a time, I delighted in keeping my home, parenting my children, and partnering with my husband. The Lord taught me during those busy days that if I'm not doing those things well, the rest of what I'm doing is *not* His will for me. The Scripture that impressed this truth on my heart was Titus 2:3–5. "Older women likewise are to be reverent in behavior, not slanderers or slaves to much wine. They are to teach what is good, and so train the young women to love their husbands and children, to be self-controlled, pure, working at home, kind, and submissive to their own husbands, that the word of God may not be reviled." Through the years, I've passed that lesson on to countless younger women, but that day in our writer's group, Kay took her place as an older woman in my life and reminded me of God's priorities.

When Charles died, Kay continued to honor her husband's leadership by finishing the writing of a Bible study series he told her to complete. Caring for him through the last year of his decline took all her time, but now she had plenty. So, Kay dove into her study of God's Word and finished that project, the last book in a series of three (*All*, *In*, and *Therefore* published by Olive Press). These three studies are the abridged version of the Bible Study she and Charles developed together titled *The Messiah Mystery*. Kay's passion is the Jewishness of our Savior and teaching the connection between the Old and New Testaments.

When I took *The Messiah Mystery* class from Kay, I heard her repeat a statement that I first heard from my dear friend Judy. Judy led me to Christ and discipled me. She, too, loved God's people, Israel, and embraced the Jewishness of our faith. "The New is concealed in the Old, and the Old is revealed in the New." I've joined Judy and Kay in the mission of reminding believers that the Bible tells *one* story—the epic of redemption. And the hero, the *Redeemer*, is Messiah Yeshua (Christ Jesus).

This year Kay's focus is to get her house in order. "I'm sifting through the shards of our life together. Sorting memorabilia that means nothing to anyone else but served as memories of our life together. I need to do this now so my children won't be burdened with cleaning out my stuff after I go on to glory," she told us one day at our writers' group.

Kay describes herself as "an alien" in this unsettling time. She feels unsettled, not only by the loss of her beloved Charlie but by the rapid decline in our culture. Many of the present changes are astounding. Technology and social norms seem to require constant upgrades. And like the atomic bomb, their potential for evil overshadows their positive usefulness. "I feel most at home in my quiet time with the Lord." She rests in the God Who does not change. He is her confidence.

Choose to be Confident

Confidence in the immutable Creator of Heaven and Earth results in humility. Only when we know Him and trust Him can we submit fully to His Sovereignty. People are more interested in being correct than being corrected. To be set straight, we first must see how broken and unrighteous we are. Yet we prefer to change the standard so we can measure up. This fickle human pride masquerades as confidence, *self-confidence.* Our pride declares we are right. Humility requires us to confess we are wrong.

God alone is righteous. And His Word sets the standard for all humanity whether they agree with Him or not. When God declares a behavior sinful, we can be confident it is a sin. When the world calls evil good and good evil, we don't have to reevaluate our position. We can humbly stand firm on the truth.

When the Supreme Court of the United States of America heard the case of Roe vs. Wade, I was only twelve and not yet a Christ-follower. I was oblivious to this landmark decision. Just four short years later, under the law's protection, I would make a horrible choice to kill my unborn child. When I came to Christ, He showed me how wrong I had been. With confidence in His standard, I can tell you abortion is murder, and the highest court in our land was wrong.

On June 25th, 2015, I went to sleep in America and woke up in Sodom. The Supreme Court redefined marriage, stating that a homosexual couple could be legally married, and all fifty states must recognize those marriages. I can tell you with confidence in the clear teaching of Scripture that homosexuality is a sin. God defines marriage as a sacred covenant between one man and one woman. Call me a homophobe. I don't care! Some people find this truth offensive. I'm afraid (with a holy fear) I have to disagree with the court's opinion, and others are free to disagree with me. Stating the truth from the Bible is different than me sharing a personal perspective. I have confidence in God's revealed truth, not my flawed notions. As a nation, we should be mindful that we have transgressed against a Holy God. Now I understand why Kay and many other God-fearing people feel like aliens in this country. This world is not our home! Can I get a witness?

As believers in Christ, we travel to Glory, pilgrims passing through on this broken trail of tears. Yet, there is joy in this journey—the joy of the Lord—our confidence and strength. As confident as I am about what God labels sin, I am equally convinced He forgives those who confess their sin. He draws near to the brokenhearted, and His mercy triumphs over judgment.

God is love, and we can be confident of His love for us. He sustains us in our pursuit to grow grand, "being *confident* of this very thing, that He who has begun a good work in you *will complete it* until the day of Jesus Christ" (Philippians 1:6).

Complete. I like the sound of that. This word communicates the idea of reaching maturity. Since you and I still live here, in this world, we know God isn't finished with us yet. We have lots of growing up to do. As we grow, let's not forget the value of remembering our past. Let's choose to record and share what we've learned with those coming behind us. Let's choose to go out and get involved in the world God loves. And *when* we face the death of those we love, let's choose to grieve with hope. Lastly, if we're going to be complete, we need the stability of a sure foundation—confidence in a never-changing standard. Grand palaces constructed on faulty foundations tumble down, like lives built on the shifting sand of human philosophies and religions. My aunt Lola was grand to me. I loved her and enjoyed spending time with her. Yet in the end, she spent her last days fearful because she never chose to build a relationship with God. Let's choose to be confident in the God Who loves us and gave Himself for us. That's Who quieted Kay's spirit. And He can hush all our concerns as well.

While having dinner in my home, my friend Shelly (also a friend of Kay's) noticed my china cabinet. "Kay Bascom has that same china hutch," she told me. Both cabinets are Kansas antiques. While I procured mine from a local antique shop, Kay inherited hers from her mother. What a blessing to own this constant, quiet, beautiful reminder of Kay. She is much like those china cabinets, beautiful in her own right yet fulfilling her purpose by displaying the treasures within—treasures gleaned through a lifetime of setting her heart on things above.

Choice Meditations

1. Read 1 Peter 1:13–16. What is holiness?

2. Consider Deuteronomy 4:9–10. How should we exercise our memory? How does communicating the work we witnessed God do in our lives benefit future generations?

3. Read 2 Timothy 1:3–7. What specific thing does Paul encourage Timothy to remember? Have you communicated your testimony of faith to your children and grandchildren?

4. Read Revelation 20:11–15. Who judges all people, and what does He evaluate?

5. Read Revelation 21:1–4. In light of this passage, what hope can we have when an unbeliever we love dies?

6. Read Psalm 138:8. How does this verse encourage you in your pursuit to grow grand?

Choice Considerations

1. Do you retell family stories, keep photo albums, or genealogies?

2. What work are you involved with outside your home and church? How are you engaging in the world around you?

3. When you experienced the death of a loved one, what

helped you through your grief? If you are currently grieving, what brings you comfort?

4. What aspects of the Bible or God's nature do you struggle to believe? When your thoughts or opinions conflict with the Bible, what do you do?

Choice Actions

1. Write out your testimony of coming to faith in Christ, then share it with someone. How old were you? Where were you? What was your life like before? How did your life change when you started following Jesus? What Bible passages played a part in your salvation?

2. Read family genealogies or memoirs. If you can't find any, you could start researching your family's past.

3. Sit down with your grandchildren and go through some old photos.

4. Pray through your photos for friends and family members from your past, thanking God for how He used them in your life.

5. Get involved in a church ministry and the community outside the church.

6. Spend time daily in God's Word and prayer to grow your confidence in Him. And watch as He grows you and makes you *grand*!

14

Meek Margaret

Living in Gentleness

"A gracious woman retains honor."
Proverbs 11:16

I beelined across the church's fellowship hall to snag a seat by Margret. "How are you doing?" I asked her.

"Fine! My ninetieth birthday is coming. My kids are planning a party. I was getting all wound up about what I wanted, then the Lord reminded me, 'It's not about you, Margaret.'"

"But it's your birthday party!"

"Yes, but all of life is about His glory—not me getting my way," she humbly reminded me.

Not My Will but Thine Be Done

Margaret taught me that dying to self is a lifelong struggle. If I want to grow grand, I must keep fighting my pride. Spiritual warfare is real. The battle rages every day. The liar whispers, "Look out for number one. You *deserve* the best of everything." Our flesh craves this deception; my flesh needs a change of diet. Let us reap the rewards of good soldiers who feed on God's truth.

That's how Margaret grew her sweet spirit. Her gentle presence draws the women of Grace like sugar attracts ants. We enjoy her company because her conversation drips with the honey of truth and wisdom.

I remember the first time I met Margaret. A mutual friend invited us for a ladies' luncheon at her home. Two things about Margaret impressed me. I confess that I don't always see people the way God does. He looks at our hearts.

On the other hand, I notice appearances first, and Margaret Landsdowne is stunning. I gaped in unbelief when she mentioned her age (at that time, 88). I've seen sixty-year-old women with more wrinkles. The few lines on her face etched evidence of a delightful countenance. Secondly, Margaret's dark eyes glistened like hot fudge. I marvel at their unaltered appearance. My mother's eyes had once been deep brown, but through the loss of pigment (a natural part of the aging process), her eyes are now a pale, muddy green. Margaret claims her eyes were once darker. But they appeared unfaded to me.

Margaret and her husband, Bob, began attending Grace Baptist Church in 1948, just one year after the church was chartered.

> "We were not charter members, but I knew them all. They're all gone now. I guess I'm the closest there is to a charter member. The church started as an outreach to the college students at K-State. We've always been mission-minded. I remember when over half of our small adult Sunday school class felt the call of God and left for mission fields around the world. We still support two of them even though they're retired. Bob said, 'If they're called to go, someone has to stay by the stuff to support them.' So that's what we did; We stayed by the stuff."

Margaret's been an *active* member of Grace for over seventy years. She's been under the leadership of several pastors through these decades and appreciates each. I have never heard her speak an ill word about anyone—especially not those the Lord appointed as leaders in the church. As the wife of her current pastor, I appreciate her respect and admiration for these men. Her refusal to gossip sets a fine example for us all. In our age of church shopping and hopping, this kind of commitment is rare, if not extinct. Margaret's church allegiance may be extinct, but she's no dinosaur. She's present and available. She no longer bears an official leadership title (though, through the years, she's had many). But Margaret Landsdowne, without a doubt, serves as the Matriarch of Grace; she's a mother and a *grand*mother to us all!

Now, at ninety-five, Margaret lives the Christ-life in a way that keeps her as new as the dawn. Yet she doesn't feel that young. On one of my recent visits, Margaret conceded that she is ready to meet the Lord and hopes He will take her home soon. Yet, despite Margaret's physical challenges (at ninety-five, she has many), she submits to the Author of Life and the days He's written for her. Her determination to live her last days as she has lived for many years—for God's glory—challenges me. Margaret shows me what true meekness looks like. Strength under control. After ninety-five years of living, Margret harbors strong opinions, but she's content to keep them to herself. She seeks God's will, not her own.

As I walked into her new apartment for my first visit with her there, I noticed a devotional with a bookmark popping up about halfway through. The title brought a smile to my face, *Sing a New Song.* I know you already heard my thoughts about this subject in Demure Doris's story, but I know as a teacher, we need to repeat and review. It's a truth that bears repeating—grand women learn new songs.

"Last Sunday, I managed to make it to Church. I really wanted to sing a familiar hymn because I didn't have the strength to stand.

When I sit, I can't see the words. I wanted to sing, but I couldn't. I'm not complaining," Margaret explained, "I know it was my problem (her will, not His). Pastor Alan always chooses music with good lyrics—sound doctrine." Margaret loves music. She spent many years at Grace Baptist Church as the choir director.

"I saw the times were changing. Music was changing. I stepped down so I wouldn't be in the way. I miss the choirs. There's a special bond in a small group of people that learn music together."

In light of Margaret's comment, you may expect her to be that cranky old lady at church who complains about the music—a worship leader's nightmare. That is *not* Margaret. "I focus on the words of new songs. Good worship music teaches us about the Lord." Margaret reminds me that style and preference have little to do with what is truly good.

It seems time affects people in one of two ways: like clay in a hot kiln, it can harden some. Others humble themselves, becoming as pliable as warm wax. Those who grow ridgid in their own opinions crack and crumble when change marches over them. But the soft souls who once stood like a tall taper, those who have let heat melt away their willfulness, become beautiful and fascinating, like sculptures of dripping wax. "The meek shall inherit the earth," Jesus said. The only difference between stubbornness and perseverance is whose will we are committed to. Mine or God's? Margaret perseveres as a meek lamb who relentlessly follows her Good Shepherd.

"I may be moving in May," Margaret disclosed. "My lease will be up, and my daughter-in-law and son have been encouraging me to move in with them for a while now."

"We're going to miss you," I lamented.

"Oh, I'm really going to miss my church family. My small group has been dear to me. I don't think I'll change my church membership. I love Grace."

"So, are you feeling you need more help?" I asked.

"Yes. I have home care twice a day, but it's expensive. My daughter often comes by, but she is in her seventies and doesn't have the strength to do all I need her to do." Margaret's daughter is the oldest of her five children. The son she spoke of is much younger. "So, as much as I would like to stay here, I believe it's time for me to move on."

Margaret hasn't moved much in her adult life. She and her husband moved to Manhattan, Kansas, just after WWII. Four of her five children were born and raised in this community. I believe she lived in two different houses before coming to her current apartment. By contrast, I've made so many moves in my life that I always wonder when the next one will be. I can't imagine how difficult it must be for Margaret. She and Bob bought their last house on the rural outskirts of town in 1979. After becoming a widow in 2012, she soon realized living that far out was unwise and moved into the same complex as her daughter.

Choose To Do Life God's Way
Margaret's my poster child for interdependence. *Interdependence* marks maturity. Independence, however, serves as a healthy phase but a horrible destination. Life is not about just taking care of ourselves. We need to care for others and know when we need others to care for us. Interdependence means we submit to meeting needs and let others meet ours.

Forsake Not the Assembling of Yourselves Together
I put off visiting Margaret entirely too long. Bill and I dropped by her house shortly after he became the pastor at Grace. We received an invitation from the care group she hosted. But after she moved, I never got around to spending time with her outside of church services. Then our Women's Ministry team decided we wanted to interview her and play the video at our annual Mission's Brunch. She greeted me at the door with her dazzling smile and welcomed me into her new place. I sat down. Her crimson sofa

with a regal gold flourish pattern reminded me of mine. I glanced around at the art on her walls; my eyes lingered on an antique print of kittens on sheet music hanging above her piano.

"Your living room reminds me of mine. You have such good taste, Margaret. And you always dress fashionably."

"Oh," she chuckles, "my daughters and granddaughters are always buying me new clothes."

"Where did the picture of the kittens come from?" I asked.

"That belonged to my mother-in-law. I always admired it."

"It's beautiful. I have antique cupid photos that belonged to my great-aunt."

"Oh, how fun."

"Were you born and raised in Kansas?" I inquire.

"Yes, I was born on the west side of the state during the dust bowl. That was quite a time. Mom kept a big sheet over the table. The food was placed under the sheet at mealtime, and you'd reach under to fix your sandwich. Then you'd take the sandwich out just long enough to take a bite. Even then, grit would grind between your teeth. There was a thick layer of dust everywhere in the house. No matter how many times a day you swept it out, it came right back in."

I continued my interview. "Sounds like a difficult time. What did your dad do for a living then?"

"Daddy was a dirt farmer. He finally saved enough to buy his own farm but lost it a year later. The drought bankrupted him. He packed us up in the car and moved us east to Altamont, Kansas. I was ten. We pulled up to a parking spot in the middle of the night. The headlights were shining on a lawn. My little brother, who was eight, sprang out the door and began rolling in the grass like a dog. He was so excited because he had never seen *green* grass before."

Our conversation reminds me of my many private history lessons over tea with Radiant Ruth forty years ago. I wonder whether my stories will keep others as riveted as these two women kept me. I studied the Dustbowl in school and even watched a good documentary shortly after moving to Kansas, but that day Margaret brought history to life, making it personal. She added texture, taste, and scent along with vibrant color. I had never imagined grass so verdant before.

As I interviewed Margaret, I learned many things. Her husband, Bob, was drafted into the army during WWII. A month after he left, she found herself pregnant with their first child despite their care to prevent it. Shortly after that, the Army notified her Bob was missing in action in Germany. She didn't know (until he arrived home at the war's end) that the Germans captured him; he spent his enlistment as a prisoner of war. Yet when I asked, "What's one of the hardest trials you ever faced?" her answer surprised me.

"When I was expecting my fourth child. I was sick most of the time and never felt good. I suffered not postpartum depression; rather, I had prenatal depression. We lived in a big stone house on Anderson out towards Keats. And one day, I heard a motorcycle pull into our driveway. I went to the door, and a teenage boy handed me a book. 'My mother told me to bring this out to you. She said that you needed it today, and you needed it now.' He faithfully conveyed his mother's message and drove away. It was a daily devotional book. I think it was July 21. So, I went to the entry for that day and read it. And it was the very Scripture verses I needed for that day. Those verses held me together that day. I hadn't had much interaction with this older woman at church. We were just acquaintances, but she knew. And she had been praying for me. And she was *obedient* to the leading of the Holy Spirit. That was one of those precious experiences that I've never forgotten."

"What did that experience teach you?"

"That if you don't have a church home, you'll miss out on an awful lot in your life. You *need* fellowship with other believers. It strengthens you."

I found Margaret's lesson instructive in two ways. First, sometimes the most difficult trials don't appear as bad as other tragedies we endure. The demons from within often inflict more pain than external circumstances. Conquering our emotions and attitudes, our pride and prejudices, requires greater stamina than going through natural disasters, pandemics, and the death of loved ones. Yet the next lesson unlocks the victory.

We cannot conquer our demons in isolation. "A man who *isolates* himself seeks his own desire; he rages against all wise judgment" (Proverbs 18:1). "Bear one another's burdens and so fulfill the law of Christ" (Galatians 6:2). God made us for Himself and each other. Man thrives in community. Christians thrive in church.

Choose to be Active in Church

John, known as the Apostle of love, makes an even stronger statement, "We know that we have passed from death to life because we love the brethren. He who does not love his brother abides in death" (1 John 3:14). When we love people, we want to be with them. We make an effort to gather. If you lack the desire to gather with other believers, John claims you are not living—you're spiritually dead. I've heard Hebrews 10:25 used like a hammer to clobber professing Christians who don't go to church: "Forsake not the assembling of yourselves together." Why do we rarely quote the positive instruction that precedes this admonition? The command is, "Let us be concerned for one another, to help one another to show love and to do good" (Hebrews 10:24, GNT). When we don't show up to spend time with one another, it reveals our lack of love. I appreciated how Margaret called this older woman's care for her an act of obedience. Because this woman obeyed the prompting of the Holy Spirit and the commands of Hebrews 10, Margaret received encouragement to keep loving her family and continue in the good work God gave her to do in her home.

Through the decades I've walked with God, I often feel His arms around me through the hug of a sister. I hear the whisper of

His wisdom from the tongues of my siblings in Christ, giving me encouragement and admonition. I've been surprised by thank you notes from others expressing their gratitude for how God spoke to them through something I said and didn't even remember saying. These things don't happen if we don't gather. To spark graciousness, to grow as a matriarch of grace, we must faithfully gather with the saints.

Through the years, I've heard many excuses from people about why they don't attend church. Frankly, most of what I hear are professions of selfishness and folly.

"My needs weren't being met." (Whose needs did you reach out to meet, I wonder).

"They were cliquish and unfriendly." (Hmm, did you ever read Proverbs 18:24, "If a man is to have friends, he must show himself friendly"? What did you do to make friends?)

"They were too friendly." (Oh, so you don't want people looking out for you?)

I could go on for pages but at the bottom line is rebellion. God is building His church. If He saved you, His will is for you to be an active member of His body. The church is not an option; it's a necessity for Christians who want to grow grand.

In Everything Give Thanks

In my recent visits with Margaret, our similarities surprised me. I confess, I kind of like the idea of being Margaret's mini-me. Her living room sofa is covered in crimson and gold. I have a chaise lounge with similar upholstery in my living room. Antique art prints hang on her walls and mine. She does jigsaw puzzles and reads good inspirational books, two of my pastimes as well. She often speaks of her family, especially her youngest great-grandson. The two of them are quite close. My kids and grandkids are also one of my favorite topics of conversation. And she eats celery and peanut butter for lunch! YUM! How many people eat celery and peanut butter for lunch? A couple of weeks after this last discovery, our visit went long. "Teri, are you getting hungry? I have celery and peanut butter."

"That sounds good. Sure, I'll join you."

She leaned forward in her recliner. Her arms tensed as she battled with gravity and arthritic pain to stand. Then she hobbled to her little kitchen. I strolled over to keep her company as she worked. As she filled the third stalk, I noticed a clear droplet forming at the tip of her nose. I hate it when that happens! I'm well on my way to being a drippy-nosed woman. But she didn't seem to notice. I snagged a tissue from the box on the counter and gently dabbed it under her nose. After all, her hands were sticky with peanut butter, and time was of the essence. She chuckled, not the least bit embarrassed. "Thank you! I didn't even feel it." She praised my humility in intervening and dealing with her bodily fluid.

"Margaret, I suspect someday I won't feel those drips coming either, and I sure hope someone dabs mine."

Margaret expresses gratitude constantly. She lives out God's will. "In everything give thanks; for this is the will of God in Christ Jesus for you" (1 Thessolonians 5:18).

It didn't surprise me to learn she lost a house in a tornado. Several in our Kansas congregation suffered homes destroyed by twisters. What did surprise me was how her husband responded to the devastation:

> "We all happened to be home together that day," Margaret began unfolding the story. "That in itself was miraculous. Our kids each had jobs and school. But when the warning siren went off, we all hunkered down in the basement together. We heard the wind roar like a freight train plowing through. We watched the roof rip off over our heads. When the dust settled, and we felt safe enough to go up, I just

gaped in unbelief. The whole house was gone. All our possessions lay scattered in every direction. I looked helplessly at my husband. 'What are we going to do, Bob?'"

"'We are all safe. We are going to get down on our knees and thank God.' And that's what we did."

Choose to be Grateful

A little appreciation goes a long way in human interactions. I remember how much doctors and nurses loved coming into my grandma Irène's hospital room because she doted over each of them with sincere gratitude. She even thanked the janitorial staff as they cleaned. "They get paid to do this," my mom would remind her. "So! I'm still glad they're doing it."

It's always more pleasant to work for people who show appreciation than those who badger us with criticism. And God feels the same way. After all, who are we to dispute how He handles the affairs of creation? "But who are you, my friend, to talk back to God? A clay pot does not ask the man who made it, 'Why did you make me like this?'" (Romans 9:20 GNT).

One of my favorite books in the Bible is the oldest one, the book of Job. Job models gratitude amid devastating circumstances. After losing all his property and children, listen to his painful response.

"Then Job arose and tore his robe and shaved his head and fell on the ground and worshiped. And he said, 'Naked I came from my mother's womb, and naked shall I return. The Lord gave, and the Lord has taken away; blessed be the name of the Lord'" (Job 2:20–21 ESV).

Then poor Job loses his health and breaks out with excruciating boils all over his body. Poor Mrs. Job is out of her mind with her grief and loss. She's had enough and can't bear to see her husband in such pain.

"Then his wife said to him, 'Do you still hold fast your integrity? Curse God and die.' But he said to her, 'You speak as one of the foolish women would speak. Shall we receive good from God, and shall we not receive evil?' In all this Job did not sin with his lips" (Job 2:9–10).

Through the furnace of affliction, Job grew grand. He credited God with every blessing and endured every burden for God's glory. Margaret and Job know the Lord with mature faith. Are we choosing to give thanks in (not for) *everything?*

Grow in the Grace and Knowledge of the Lord

"Margaret, how old were you when you came to know Jesus?"

"I asked Jesus to be my Savior when I was about ten. But to really *know* Him, that wasn't until later. But I always wanted to please God because I grew up in a Christian home. Sometimes that's a hindrance when you grow up with it. You have to find out later on God doesn't have any grandchildren. Getting to know Jesus never ends. You continue to grow in your walk with the Lord. He becomes more precious as the years go by. Especially, when you look back and see He was there with you all the time."

Choose to Grow Spiritually

Margaret misses her garden and the big picture window facing westward, where she and Bob enjoyed watching the sunset. But she never misses breakfast with Jesus. Margaret starts her day with prayer and time in her Bible. Some Sundays, she watches the live stream from Grace when she's too weak to go to church. She still plays private concerts on her piano for her King; Margaret sings for His glory, and He is honored by her worship. God's economy is full of paradoxes. To live, you must die. To grow up, you must become a child.

I remember coming to the revelation that as I grew older, God seemed bigger. Here's the entry from my journal.

May 29, 2008

(the day after my 47th birthday)

The older I get, the more I realize how little I know. Even though I'm constantly learning new things, I have become increasingly aware of my ignorance. As I grow in knowledge, the incomprehensible expanse we call omniscience seems to grow more rapidly. As I fill my finite brain with new facts or grasp new understanding, my awareness of the infinite becomes more acute. In the attempt to reach the limits of my potential, haphazard as it may be, I'm increasingly aware that there is far more beyond my limits than I can imagine. I grow, and God "grows" (at least my perception of Him grows). I do not know what the future holds, but I know Who holds the future! This simple, finite creature takes great comfort in this reality.

I believe this is the secret of Margaret's youthful appearance—her childlike adoration of her Heavenly Father. The more birthdays she celebrates, the more her reliance on God develops. Unlike biological children who must grow from dependence to independence and finally into interdependence, God's children begin as independent sinners. We, as sinful people, must learn interdependence in a spiritual community and grow to complete dependence on God. Margaret knows her Father, the Ancient of Days and understands that by comparison, she is just an infant.

"Let the little children come unto me for such is the kingdom of Heaven." ~ Jesus

C.S. Lewis writes about this phenomenon in *the Lion, the Witch, and the Wardrobe*:

"Aslan," said Lucy, "you're bigger."

"That is because you are older, little one," answered he.

"Not because you are?"

"I am not. But every year you grow, you will find me bigger."

Choice Meditations

1. The first mention of the church in the New Testament is Matthew 16:18. Who mentions it, and what promise is given?

2. Read Acts 2:40–47. How did the Lord fulfill His promise in Matthew 16:18? What does this reveal about God's will concerning His followers and church?

3. What do you discover about God's will for you in

1 Thessalonians 5:1–8? How does this relate to your involvement in church? How does this relate to developing an attitude of gratitude?

4. As you read 1 John 1:12–14, what do you find about the stages of spiritual growth? Describe the circular progression to dependence on God.

Choice Considerations

1. What area in your life do you know is not pleasing to God? What makes obedience to His will for you in this matter so difficult?

2. How active are you in church? Do you have close relationships with any people you attend church with? If not, what can you do to find a good friend in your church?

3. Listen to your conversations with others. How frequently do you express thankfulness to them and God?

4. How have you tasted the goodness of God? Does your appetite for understanding the Bible, His Word, resemble a hungry infant? (1 Peter 2:2–3)

Choice Actions

1. Plan and take one step of obedience to God's revealed will (you read it in the Bible) for you.

2. Pray for people you go to church with, and choose one thing you can do to encourage another church member.

3. Begin and end your day with thanksgiving. Before you get

out of bed, thank God for the day. When you get into bed, thank God for specific blessings from the day.

4. Keep a journal. Record what you learn about God as you read the Bible. Record what you discover about His will (what He wants you to do). Share at least one lesson a week from your journal with someone else so they can be encouraged to know the Lord!

15

Embracing Winter's Beauty
Conclusion

"To everything there is a season,
A time for every purpose under heaven."
Ecclesiastes 3:1

F all depresses me. I know some people, like my husband, love it. For me, however, autumn means the end of summer's warmth and sunshine. The long-lit days of working in my yard, cooking outside on the grill, and swimming in my pool—those days have passed. I spent most of my growing-up years in southern places close to the beach, South Carolina, San Diego, and Guam. I grew up grooving to the good vibrations of the Beach Boys, and *Endless Summer* (the title of one of their better-known albums) became my mantra. Like the Coppertone baby, I sported a fabulous tan line above my ivory bottom all summer long. These days it's a little higher since I wear a one-piece or tankini, but my olive skin rarely burns and doesn't require much sun to turn brown. Yup, I love summer.

Most women love the summer of life. Those young adult years are when we've gained independence and begun to run our households. During this season, our bodies are firm and strong. Our faces gleam with smooth, supple skin. Our hair lacks those pesky silver strands. Some of us bear children and enjoy the feelings of a separate life inside us. Some of us pursue careers and feel empowered to change the world. These years exude possibility and promise, but they are short. It may feel like forever if you're in them. Will the baby ever sleep so I can? Will I ever get that promotion? Yes. Then you'll wake up to teenagers and/or the responsibilities and demands of a successful career. You'll look wearily in the mirror and see a stranger with lines on her face and sagging appendages. Fall has arrived, and you realize winter comes next. Can we find ardor in these seasons when our outer strength and beauty fade so quickly?

Those who love the change of seasons know we can. The cool temperatures and vibrant colors of fall delight us. Winter wonderlands gleam with brilliance; ice and snow sparkle. So, these later seasons of life hold particular loveliness all their own. These are the seasons of *grand* and *great.* Yet if we lament too long for past seasons, we miss the opportunity to embrace the delight of the next one.

Grand Flexpectations

Have you ever gathered firewood? I bet you didn't go trying to snap the live limbs of living trees. You looked for the dead, dry sticks, right? The funny thing about trees in the winter is their branches don't look much different than the dead limbs on the ground, but just try snapping one off. You'll soon discover they're quite alive and won't break easily. Those branches that look dead flex with the weight of snow and ice. They may bend, but they resist breaking. Living things keep growing and maintain flexibility. Deadwood burns well, but it can never again bloom or bear fruit.

From the Idaho Mountain Express, June 16, 2006. An interview with Alba Arndt (my great-aunt of chapter 7).

"Change is an inevitable part of life," she pointed out.

In one of her favorite books—"The Thorn Birds" by Colleen McCullough, written in 1977—Arndt likes a passage where a mother is speaking to her son about change.

"You must accept change. You will be a better man," the mother says to her son in the book.

The quote rings true for Arndt.

"Otherwise, you'll make yourself miserable," she said. "That's been a quote for me ever since."

Remembering Alba was a librarian, I suspect she read that book the year it came out. She was sixty-seven in 1977 and ninety-four at the publication of this interview. Alba realized the importance of flexibility. She chose to bend, not break. Heat hardens clay and melts wax. Time is like a furnace to our souls; some harden and become brittle, fragile, and ugly. Others retain their elasticity, stretching, growing more potent, and revealing a better beauty, a lasting beauty. The women in this book owned that charm. Like the woman of valor in Proverbs 31:21, these women were prepared for the winter of life. "She is not afraid of snow for her household, for all her household are clothed in scarlet." Have we clothed ourselves and our households in scarlet? Are we bracing ourselves for the inevitability of winter?

Bracing for Winter's Bitter Cold

Courage. How many times did you hear that word in this book? At least twelve, I'm sure. Getting old isn't for cowards. Cold places require courage. Three of the most fridged locations known to man are outer space, Antarctica, and the grave. Whether we're the astronaut exploring space, the scientist researching the South Pole, or the person living in a body nine decades nearer the grave, we can't do it without courage. Winter's most delectable delights are only enjoyed by those courageous enough to brave the cold. There's a reason the elderly set their thermostats at eighty degrees; they're feeling the winter of life. Their skin has thinned. Their fatty layer dissipates. Their circulation slows down. I remember asking my great-grandmother Rose Anna, "Do you go outside much?"

"Oh no," she told me, "It hurts. The breeze hurts my skin." She was ninety-seven at the time. This woman who once enjoyed cultivating roses could no longer brave the elements. Her body was wearing out, but her spirit retained strength, and she learned to find new simple pleasures in the nursing home, despite her blindness and bedridden state. Rose Anna had flexed and, at the same time, chose to keep a positive outlook on her life. She kept choosing to do right.

I hope our resolve to do right hardens like water to ice. Today I saw that resolve on my friend Mary Anne's face.

Mary Anne's Move

Spotting the U-Haul truck, we drove up to Mary Anne's. Brothers from the church toted loads out the door and up the truck ramp. My husband doesn't show up to every move at our church, but this one was special. We needed to say goodbye to a dear sister. Mary Anne, now in her eighties, had been an active member of Grace Baptist Church long before Bill and I came. She prepared well for moving. Her two-bedroom duplex echoed with emptiness as we entered. It hadn't taken long to pack up her place. We found Mary Anne inside directing the crew.

"Here are some quilts and blankets to protect the wood furniture. Teri, would you take them to the guys loading up?"

"Sure!" I answered, reaching for the bundle.

Mary Anne and I enjoyed our last visit together as the move continued. Her voice rang out pleasantly as she switched between conversation and directing traffic. I watched the gears turn in her head through the window of her eyes, revealing the thousands of moving details Mary Anne juggled. What grace she carried those details out with. I need to learn that skill. I am not always so pleasant under stressful circumstances.

My thoughts returned to a conversation she and I had at church about three or four months before. We were discussing the recent move of her dearest friend, Dorothy.

"Dorothy wants to come back here, but I don't think it will happen. She just can't live alone anymore." Mary Anne stated matter-of-factly. She continued, "I'll be seventy-nine this year. I think it's time for me to move closer to my kids too. I'm visiting my daughter in Lincoln, Nebraska, next week. She and I will start looking at places for me to go."

And now she was on her way. I mentioned in the first section of this book what a blessing to our family it has been that both of my grandmothers and my mom knew what Mary Anne did. I worry about people who don't want to do anything until they have no other option. Will they realize they can't take care of themselves? Who will have to put a foot down and say sorry, it's time—you *need* to leave your home? Or will one of their children be burdened with daily visits? I pray I will have the courage to be grand and give up my notions of independence. I want to remember what I tried hard to teach my children when they were teens, "Independence is not maturity. I'm glad you can take care of yourself. There are hundreds of homeless teens on the streets of Portland doing just that. They are not mature. Maturity is *inter*dependence; it's understanding your place in the community. Not just taking care of yourself but taking care of others and *knowing when you need them to take care of you.*"

May the Lord help us to know when we need to be cared for and to take care of others by submitting to that reality with a gracious attitude.

Some were quiet. Some were bold. All were grand. None were old.

The shadows of Radiant Ruth and Legendary Lola loom over me, along with the clouds of the other grand women I've known, many of whom I don't mention in this book. I cower under my memories of these women, overwhelmed by how they lived so well at the end of a long life. I feel insecure in my attempt to do the same. I've heard that the days are long, but the years are short.

My own experience confirms this statement. My fifty-plus years rushed past, but today seems to drag. This day drags like the night I rocked a sick infant or the day I spent toilet training a toddler. Today creeps at a glacier's pace, just like when I discovered my fifteen-year-old daughter skipped school; her boyfriend took her to an R-rated movie. The day my college freshman called from a hospital on the opposite side of the country to tell me she had been in a car accident was another slow grinding day. The most challenging days seem to drag on while fun, exciting days streak like lightning bolts.

Today, much like yesterday, I find myself fighting fatigue. Though I confess, yesterday I lost the fight and took a nap. I find myself lost in a murky malaise. Where did my zest go? I need to find the spice of life right now because mine tastes bland. Can you relate? I hope not!

For those of us who know depression, there are days that death doesn't sound bad. I remember my friend Cindy's description, "There are days when I take a shower, and I just want to turn into water and run down the drain."

I have battled depression since childhood. Over twenty years ago, God granted me a decisive victory in understanding how to fight depression, but since menopause, depression has implemented a new weapon in the arsenal—fatigue. Shortly after I went through the change, convinced my thyroid must be off, I made an appointment with my doctor. He ran lots of blood work. "Everything looks great," he assured me.

"So, I'm just getting old, fat, and tired?"

"That would be it," my doctor chuckled.

"Thanks!" My reply seethed with sarcasm.

As I talked with my peers, I realized fatigue in this stage of life is common. So, I put on my big girl panties, swallowed mega doses of vitamin B, and got on with life. I lost fifteen pounds and seemed to be living again. Then in August of 2015, a heart attack blindsided me. Fatigue reached a new low; I continued to slug it out. Yes, I attempt regular exercise and a healthy diet, but let's face it, girlfriend, life gets crazy sometimes, and the best plan A turns into plan C or Z in a blink of an eye. My plan A had been to submit a proposal for this book by September 2015. The stress of self-imposed deadlines halted that plan and put me on a new timeline.

"Fatigue makes cowards of us all," Vince Lombardi, the famous coach of the Green Bay Packers, once told his team. Yet he led them to five national championships in seven years. That's the coward I need to be, the one who keeps fighting to win. Healthy, living things battle for life. When I'm not healthy is when I want to die.

Fatigue and depression are the enemies of the elderly. Some women who've never been depressed a day in their young lives suffer depression for the first time in their eighties or nineties. One of America's founding fathers, John Quincy Adams, suffered a stroke late in life and never fully recovered. A friend inquired about his health, to which Adams replied, "I inhabit a weak, frail, decayed tenement; battered by the winds and broken in upon by the storms, and from all I can learn, the landlord does not intend to repair." We, too, inhabit failing bodies. We must discover how to thrive or at least keep living with compromised physical and mental health. On days I feel like going to sleep and not waking up, I hear Louise Scholes rebuking me, "Live as long as you're alive!"

So, why was I feeling so low? I looked in the wrong place. I was looking inward, not upward and outward. I felt overwhelmed by comparing myself to others instead of looking to the God Who made me who I am for His purpose. I felt a need for achievement rather than resting in the reality that God would complete the work He began in me. He has good things for me to accomplish, but that work doesn't make me His beloved child. I'm already seated with Him in heavenly places. He calls me to these tasks for *His* glory, *not* mine. And by His grace, I'll keep living for His glory, one choice at a time.

Choices

Thirty-five choices! That's how many specific choices I've talked about in this book. That's a lot to think about—overwhelming even. Yet we make hundreds of choices daily, some without even thinking. They're more habit. Habits that result from making the same choices over and over again. I'm sure you have already chosen to do several of the things I've discussed. You've formed some good habits. I'm sure not all of you are slackers like me. You work hard. It's who you are—you're industrious. Cross that off. Once you have identified who you've already chosen to be, pick one or two choices you want to make to develop your character. Poor habits will never change if we don't stop and think about what we're doing. And to be honest, we need to change some of our practices. I imagine this list as a giant peach (like the one in James's adventure) because eating elephants **is** *not* tempting. I'm going to gobble down these delicious qualities one at a time until the sweetness of each transforms my disposition. If it makes it any easier, remember that these choices *reflect the nature of God*, whose image we should bear.

1. God is light.

2. God uses color intentionally.

3. God created us to cultivate creativity.

4. God values a gentle and quiet spirit because He is gentle.

5. God balances joy and sorrow.

6. God is flexible. He completes His work no matter how

much sin and Satan try to mess Him up.

7. God takes the initiative.

8. God is generous.

9. God takes an interest in people.

10. God chooses true wealth (friends).

11. God celebrates life. JUBILEE!

12. God rules and grants us dominion.

13. God is skillful.

14. God is tenacious.

15. God is brave.

16. God is prepared.

17. God is friendly and approachable.

18. God doesn't need practice because He is perfect. So, we practice getting closer to perfect.

19. God not only built a bridge in time but beyond time. His bridge leads to eternity!

20. God's Word is always relevant.

21. God shares and teaches us good things because He is good.

22. God does not complain. He does rightfully execute Judgement.

23. God is committed to His children.

24. God laughs.

25. God is beautiful, inside and out.

26. God is discreet—He covers our sins.

27. God enjoys new songs.

28. God has preserved His history of redemption in the Bible.

29. God is humble. The Creator of the universe died as a thief on a cross.

30. Jesus is the Prince of Peace!

31. God is Confident.

32. God always accomplishes His will; why not just cooperate?!

33. The church is His Body; the heart of Christ beats there.

34. Gratitude is a hallmark of God's children.

35. God is Spirit; let's seek to expand our capacity to know Him. According to the Westminster Shorter Catechism, "The chief end of man (humankind) is to glorify God and enjoy Him forever."

Grand souls make others feel grand. They empower us, challenge us, and encourage us. That's what these women did for me. That's what I want to do for women coming after me. Isn't that what you want too? Let's commit to making godly choices, *grand* choices. And *when* (not if) age afflicts our bodies with unpleasant changes, let's echo my grandma, Irène, "C'est la vie!" Let's grow grand, *not* old.

A Word From the Author:

"Thank you so much for joining me on this glorious adventure to grow grand! I invite you to join me in my home on the internet. Just scan the QR code, and you'll be there. I offer free gifts to all and a hidden page of freebies to my subscribers that includes free PDFs of the Steeped In Truth Bible Studies. You'll also find information about my next book projects and discover a few of my favorite books. Have a blessed-beyond-measure life!"

†eri Gasser

SCAN ME

Made in the USA
Monee, IL
12 June 2023

35546919R00149